I'd Still
Choose
You

DRAGONFLY PUBLISHING
Collegeville, Pennsylvania

ISBN:

eBook	979-8-9899964-1-4
Paperback	979-8-9899964-0-7
LCCN	2024901715

First Edition
Book Production and Publishing by Brands Through Books
brandsthroughbooks.com

Cover photo by *Memories by Maria Photography*, used with permission.

www.rebeccaditore.com
www.smallmomentsfoundation.org

I'd Still Choose *You*

A Young Widow's Journey of
Unconditional Love, Deep Grief,
and Life After Loss

Rebecca DiTore

DRAGONFLY
PUBLISHING

Praise for I'd Still Choose You

While I have heard, "It is better to have loved and lost than never to have loved at all," throughout my life, never have I truly understood the depth and honesty of those words until reading *I'd Still Choose You* by Rebecca DiTore.

In Rebecca's debut book, a memoir about the love, life, and loss of her husband, she takes her readers on a heartbreaking yet inspiring journey. She gifts her readers the raw pain and the unfiltered beauty.

Written as not just the telling of her circumstances but as a gentle guide to assist those in similar situations, Rebecca offers suggestions and helpful hints along the way.

I'd Still Choose You is one woman's awe-inspiring answer to the age-old question: Is love worth the pain?

This reader knows the answer!

LISA N. PAUL, Amazon best-selling author

Rebecca's story and her ability to tell it in such a brave and honest way make this book a must-read for anyone experiencing grief. Although my personal story of loss is very different from Rebecca's, it left me with grief that will never fully leave me. I have found love, joy, and fulfillment, but simultaneously, I grieve.

Through my work at the Breathing Room Foundation, I often witness deep grief when our recipients experience loss, and I believe this perspective will be of great value to them.

I found Rebecca's words to be raw and heartbreaking, funny and validating, relatable and hopeful, uplifting and inspiring. Her words will be a gift to anyone experiencing grief, whether recent or lifelong, giving guidance and permission to open your heart, without guilt, so that you can live a fulfilling and joyful life.

MARY ELLEN FITZGERALD, bereaved sister and executive director of the Breathing Room Foundation

"Where there is life and there are options, there is hope." A direct quote from the book *I'd Still Choose You* and the epitome of what the writing is about. When her world shatters in the face of the harsh reality that her twenty-nine-year-old husband, Mike, has aggressive brain cancer, author Rebecca DiTore does everything in her power to save her husband and the father of her two young sons. Rebecca remains steadfast in her hope that her husband will defy all the odds and have many more years with their family. When love and hope aren't enough to save her husband and she becomes a young widow, Rebecca's hope turns toward creating a peaceful life with her two boys—a life where grief and joy can coexist. In this beautifully honest memoir, Rebecca demonstrates the power of holding out faith that there is a light to be found at the end of any dark tunnel. She exemplifies resilience and love in the face of the unimaginable and demonstrates that no matter what life throws at you, there still can be meaning to be found and a beautiful life to be lived.

WHITNEY LYN ALLEN, author of *Running in Trauma Stilettos* and certified grief educator

I'd Still Choose You is a book that reaches your very core. Rebecca shares her heartbreaking journey as a young woman and mother going through an unbelievable time. As I read this book, going through my own family's struggle with losing my spouse, I actually felt like the book was written for me. Rebecca's words validated my anticipatory grieving and left me feeling like I was no longer alone. This is a must-read book if you have gone or are going through severe grief of a loved one. There's joy in the stories of her children and heartache in her grief, but in the end, you will truly feel like you are not alone.

JILL WELLER, middle school secretary and widow

Rebecca bravely shares her heart-wrenching journey as a young widow and caregiver, navigating the devastating effects of brain cancer on her family. We often hear the first person account of treatment from the patient's experience. The role of caregiver is often more mentally taxing; her raw and honest account offers a glimpse into the profound challenges she faced while caring for her husband with their two young children at home. Touched with humor, *I'd Still Choose You* is a powerful testament to love, loss and the strength of family and provides hope and validation to anyone experiencing grief.

DONALD CARLINO, 2x cancer survivor and American Cancer Society advocate

To Michael Louis DiTore, the first love of my life,
You taught me true unconditional love. Your love gave me so much happiness, followed by the deepest sorrow we can feel in our human experience. But in the end, the pain is worth every second I had with you and every second I have with our sweet boys, who remind me of you every single day.

Thank you for encouraging me to pursue my dream of this book, knowing you wouldn't be here to hold it in your hands. You were a real and rare example of selflessness.

I've heard that grief is the continuation of love. It serves as proof that love was here, and I suppose if that's true, then I welcome my grief, because our love was a gift. I hope you know from the clouds that in every lifetime, in any universe, if I was told the ending of our story and had a chance to do it all over, without hesitation, I'd still choose you.

To Dante and Dominic.
I'm not sure you will ever understand the healing power you two have. Your love, affection, and innocence quite literally saved my life. I know there is a dull ache in your hearts. One that I can't fix. But you, without question, have so much of your daddy inside you. I promise you, with every bit of my heart, that I will do everything in my power to support you through your journeys as you navigate your own grief.

I hope this book shows you who Mike DiTore was—as a person, as a partner, and as a father. I hope this book shows you your own strength and enlightens you about the battles you've already overcome in your short lives, reminding you that you can get through hardship if you allow yourself to be vulnerable and move forward with love and gratitude.

"I am strong. I am smart. I am kind. I am loved and I can do hard things!" These are a few words we say together each night before bed. I need you to continue to believe in them every day of your life—just as you do now at three and four years old. There aren't words in the English dictionary that can properly convey the magnitude of my love for you. You are my entire world, and this book, my sweet boys, above all else, is for you.

Contents

Letter to My Reader

IT WAS A HOT SUMMER MORNING IN JUNE OF 2018 WHEN MY husband, Mike, and I were walking across the train tracks from our townhome in Pennsylvania to the Penndale Middle School parking lot, where the Lansdale Farmers' Market was held each week. With one hand, Mike was holding the blue leash of our black lab, Wesley Hutch DiTore. With his other hand, he held onto one of mine.

We frequented this farmers' market, but this day, in particular, stands out—our conversation surrounded our recent pregnancy news. We talked about our unborn child. Our son. We talked about what he would be like and what he would look like. We talked about how lucky our son would be, along with his future life partner, to grow up with Mike as his role model. We talked about the positive impact it would have on him to hear the way Mike spoke to me and see the way he treated me—to see a strong, healthy relationship with mutual respect and appreciation for one another. We talked about how special it would be that our son and other future children would get to grow up witnessing a love story as unique and true as ours.

That, at least, was what we expected.

A few years and two children later, that future we talked about on our walk to the farmers' market was ripped out from under us with one simple word: cancer.

When Mike was first diagnosed, I felt numbness and shock, helplessness and anger. A cure did not exist, and for that reason, I felt like both our lives were ending. His death would come from this illness. Mine, from heartbreak.

In the early days of Mike's diagnosis, I truly felt that there was no possible way that I could go on in this life without him. If you're reading this, it's likely that you're feeling a similar sentiment about your own trauma. Maybe you're in the depths of grief. Maybe you're anticipating a loss or you're in the very thick of caregiving. Maybe you've already said goodbye to your person. Maybe you feel as though you're barely hanging on. Those complex feelings, coupled with the love and connection I've found through blogging my own journey, have inspired me to write this book. Because while I can't promise you that all of the unbearable feelings that you're feeling will go away indefinitely, I can promise you that this will get easier. I can promise you that you are not alone. And I can promise you that reclaiming joy is possible.

Throughout this book, we'll talk about the ebbs and flows of grief. You'll see how my life got flipped upside down and how every plan and dream I ever had was imploded in front of me by that ugly word, cancer.

But through my grief, I've discovered a sense of peace and purpose that I'd never felt before. When we least expect it, life just happens. And sometimes, the only thing we can control is how we react to what comes our way.

For someone who literally plans to make plans, my life hasn't gone at all as planned. You see, when I was a young teen and I envisioned my adult life, I saw two or three kids, a traditional family life, a nice home, a yard, and a dog (a Labrador, to be specific). I saw a kitchen table where the four or five of us sat down for dinner each night and talked about our day. I saw my mom at the other end of the phone whenever I had a question, like, "Mom, Dominic's poop is green, but he didn't eat anything green. So what's wrong with him? Oh, and while I have you on the phone, how the heck do I actually get him to eat something green?!" I saw my husband and I growing old together, walking hand in hand on the Ocean City, New Jersey, boardwalk with our grandkids. Three generations. A big ol' happy family. No sad stuff here.

As you've probably collected by now, that teenage vision isn't how my life panned out. As I write this book, the reality of my adult life is that I'm a thirty-two-year-old motherless widow with two young boys and no ability to shoot a text up to my mom in heaven to ask about sleep disruptions or toddler belly aches or green poops.

Saying my life has been anything but what I expected is the understatement of a lifetime. While I am all those things just shared, I'm also content, independent, fulfilled, and strong as hell. I actually feel joy, which is different from just happiness. Happiness depends on external factors—a man, a vacation, or clothes might bring you happiness. But that happiness is fleeting. Joy, though? Joy is truly being at peace. Letting go of what you can't control. Pursuing your passion. Understanding who you are and what your purpose is. That's joy. And no one can take that away from you.

Am I complete? No. There is a massive piece of my heart missing, replaced with a persistent ache that will linger for the rest of my days. But despite the reality of the gnawing emptiness, I am at peace.

In May of 2021, when I heard that ugly word cancer for the first time in reference to my husband, I truly never thought feeling anything but sorrow would ever be possible again. My life today is far from what I expected. But you know what? I will still be okay.

I remember sitting at the table at a friend of a friend's apartment with a mic in front of me on a random Tuesday summer night in 2023, recording a podcast for the very first time.

"Damn, life threw you lemons, and you made this huge freaking decadent lemon meringue pie!" said one of the co-hosts after I had poured my entire life trajectory out to an audience I knew very little about.

I just shared the greatest devastation of my life; how is that what you picked up on? I thought.

But as I sit here and ponder my life, I can say with certainty that there are still a lot of decadent parts to it. It feels as if I went into the kitchen to bake this delicious cashew pie (it's totally a thing; in fact, it was my late husband's request for every holiday and birthday) but accidentally followed the wrong recipe. And when the oven beeped, my cashew pie was actually a lemon meringue pie. It's not what I asked for. It's not what I intended to make. Some of the pie was extra sour, but the other pieces turned out pretty damn delicious.

That's my life for you. Sweet and sour and unintended. It's nowhere near perfect. But what is?

I want you to know that you, too, will make a lemon meringue pie—or an apple pie; or a pumpkin pie; or, depending on your allergies, perhaps a cashew pie—from the crappy ingredients you have at your disposal. Life will inevitably be filled with ups and downs, but despite your pain, you, too, can still have a great deal of peace and joy.

So, my reader, my goal with this book is to help you feel validated in your grief and to give you hope that you, too, will slowly rise from this very dark place you might find yourself in today. I thank other widows who walked this path before me, as they gave me the validation and hope that I needed. My goal is to be that person for you.

CHAPTER 1

Mr. Sullivan's Eighth-Grade Math Class

MY HUSBAND WAS MY PARTNER IN EVERY ASPECT OF MY LIFE. He was my co-parent. My companion. My childhood best friend. My biggest fan. My sounding board. The first love of my life. We grew up together, and by doing so, we had an intense dependence on each other. I depended on him financially after our kids were born, as we decided it was best for our family that I cut back on working full-time to be home with our kids. I depended on him for reprieves from parenting, moments of self-care, a few extra minutes of sleep, laughs, support, and adventures. Healthy or not, I literally depended on him for my happiness.

I'm a different person today than I was in my marriage, but neither now nor in my marriage could I ever remember who I was before Mike. There was no Becca without Mike. It had always been Mike and Becca since we were teenagers. When I go back to that vision—the teenage me picturing my future and my dream of becoming a wife and mother—it all became so much more tangible after meeting my husband back in grade school.

* * *

My family moved to Horsham, Pennsylvania, when I entered the sixth grade. It was minimally disruptive. I made friends quickly but still envied the kids who had the opportunity to grow up together, the friends who met back in kindergarten and stuck together. Middle school is such a difficult time in child development. Kids were mean—and I mean truly *ruthless*. I had my fair share of insecurities and embarrassment. The trials and tribulations of my middle school days, however, could be a plot for an entirely separate book.

It was in Mr. Sullivan's eighth-grade math class that this super cute boy about five feet nine with a chubby stature, a face full of metal, and hair that should have been cut two years prior swept me off my feet. I can picture him in his green polo and neon Bathing Ape sneakers. He used words too sophisticated for a middle schooler and had the most genuine kindness about him. He was the kid who was friends with everyone and disliked by no one. He was easygoing and outgoing. Turns out that I, an Aéropostale fashionista with my jean cuffs tucked behind the thick tongues of my DC shoes, swept him off his feet as well. Middle school *was* hard, but it was also where I met my husband, the shiniest, silver-est lining of all silver linings.

Come high school the following year, Mike asked me to our ninth-grade homecoming dance. We awkwardly danced and slow danced, and during "Dreaming of You" by Selena, he popped the question. "Will you be my girlfriend?" he asked. So, on November 18, 2006, at the wee age of fifteen, Mike DiTore and I officially became *a thing*. And so, this date became our official *date-aversary*.

From that day on, we couldn't go even one class without seeing each other. We'd spend our weekends at the local Regal, dropped off by our parents, of course. I'd sit through his baseball games holding up a sign—"Go #25!"—and we'd walk around at every high school football game together. We'd go on long walks at the nearby parks. We'd coordinate a bathroom break at the same time so we could sneak a quick kiss at the lockers. He'd walk me to every class, and we'd write notes back and forth all day long, like this one that I pulled straight from my closet stash:

Michael,

These past two years were so amazing, and I can't even begin to describe them here, but I will try my best. :) I am so thankful to have met you. All the way back in eighth grade is crazy to think about. I was so shy we couldn't even talk on the phone! The eighth-grade picnic, the movies, the Phillies games, or how about the six million times you asked me out, and everything else back when we were so weird, haha! The trips to the beach, watching your baseball games, driving with no destination, meeting between classes, constant texting, and waiting for each other in our cars. I just want you to know that I am the happiest, luckiest girl in the world. You mean everything to me! You are the love of my life, and I'd be lost without you. I never want to know what that feels like. Thank you for the best two years of my life. We have many more to come.
Love Always & Forever,
Rebecca Leigh a.k.a Becky a.k.a Bec a.k.a Becky Bop

Hey Becky!
All my classes are going SO slow today! Especially Spanish class! This semester has gone by so quick, and we're going to have different classes and new meeting spots. Saturday will be a lot of fun. Everyone is getting dressed up and all. I'm not sure what to wear.

Like, what kind of pants? Anyway, time for me to pay attention! Love ya, babe!

Mikey,
You're always there for me when I need you, and if I could spend every second with you, I would . . . okay, well, I'll see you in like five minutes when class is over!

First of all, *crinnnnnnge.*

We were completely crazy about each other. Annoyingly inseparable, some might have said at the time. No one really expected this high school fling to last, though. I mean, what were the odds?

Actually, I will tell you.

The Hive Law, a company that supports legal needs such as estate planning, evaluated data on relationships from a Stanford study of four thousand people. This data showed that less than 2 percent of people marry their first love, and for every one hundred high school sweethearts, two go on to get married. If you're one of those big dreamers who believe that a relationship can last the test of time after high school, you should know that 37 percent of long-distance relationships end in the first semester of college.[1]

I knew it, though. I knew back in eighth grade, even before our official *date-aversary,* that we'd easily fit into that small percentage. I knew we'd prevail through every hiccup we'd encounter in college and beyond.

As I went off to Saint Joseph's University in Philadelphia, Pennsylvania, and Mike went off to Seton Hall University in South Orange, New Jersey, we were met with new challenges—another expectation mismatch.

Mike did, in fact, break up with me in that first semester of college. There was no more walking each other to class or passing notes back and forth. We no longer lived just six minutes from each other. The separate lives and new dynamic caused college to be a difficult adjustment for us.

When Mike broke up with me, I was absolutely devastated. He had become such an integral part of every single piece of my life. I was left heartbroken in a new school with new people who couldn't have possibly known the history he and I had.

It wasn't *just another breakup.*

My freshman roommate, Brooklynne, whom I'd only known in person for about two weeks at the time, tried to step in and console me. In fact, she played a pretty significant role both times my life fell apart because of Mike. You'll hear more about that later on, though.

Brooke brought me food from Campion (our school cafe) because I didn't want to leave the room, and I sure as hell didn't want to eat.

It is said that there are five stages of grief: denial, anger, bargaining, depression, and acceptance. We'll discuss them later on, but it's important to know that you don't only grieve when a person physically dies. In addition to the stages of grief, I want you to remember the term *anticipatory grief*, as we'll talk about its significance later on.

After we broke up, I grieved a relationship with my very best friend and the comfort, safety, and security that came along with that. I grieved the future I thought we'd have together.

When my breakup grief moved to the anger phase, Brooke played songs like "I Look So Good Without You" by Jessie James Decker and "Summer Girl" by Leighton Meester. We'd jump and dance on our beds, screaming Leighton's lyrics about not needing boyfriends because we had amazing girl-friends. It was our "I don't need a man!" era, and we had so much fun in it.

But in the end, I did. I totally needed my boyfriend back. I knew he wasn't *just* a boyfriend. He was my future husband and the father of my future children. My eighth-grade self would have told you the very same thing. Our breakup only lasted a month, but you better believe I held it over Mike's head our entire relationship (in the utmost endearing way, of course).

Once we were back together, we were determined to make the distance between us less trying. It took Mike approximately four hours to travel by train from South Orange, New Jersey, to Philadelphia, Pennsylvania, to visit me in college—South Orange to Secaucus Junction to Newark to 30th Street to Overbrook. He did this trip *countless* times. Some were planned, and I'd pick him up at the train station. Other times, he'd surprise me at my door.

The rest of our college years were spent intertwining our two new lives. I became best friends with his new best friends and vice versa. We attended sorority date parties and formals and had too many nights dancing and wobbling through Manayunk. We took our first official vacation alone to Clearwater, Florida, to see a Phillies spring training game (*go sports!*). And I spent countless nights in a dirty apartment with him and his roommates, an apartment that smelled like a mix of sweat, farts, and beer and was decorated with stolen street signs and empty beer boxes.

Our new lives intertwined so naturally. If that very brief breakup taught us anything, it was that we couldn't live without each other, that is, until living without each other was the only choice we had.

CHAPTER 2

The One Where Rebecca Has Her Baby

AFTER COLLEGE, MIKE AND I WENT ON TO GET ENGAGED AND married, both in Ocean City, New Jersey, the very same place I'd later stand by myself at the edge of the water to spread my husband's ashes into the Atlantic. I'd paint you an emotional picture in which tears were running down my face, but the truth is that I was too numb to comprehend what the sand-like pieces sifting through my fingers actually were.

After exchanging vows and celebrating our love as husband and wife, we rescued our Labrador, Wesley, and moved into our first home, a townhome we built in Lansdale, Pennsylvania, about forty minutes outside of Philadelphia.

It was all happening. My dreams were being realized. Every expectation of the life I imagined was being met. Life was a fairy tale!

We went on our dream trip to Italy for our first wedding anniversary and then, a few months later, decided to grow our family. It just so happened that during our very first attempt at baby-making back in 2018, the *Friends* Season 8 finale was on in the background in our room. Rachel and Ross were in the hospital waiting to deliver. I will forever connect the theme song of *Friends* with me laying on our bed with my legs straight up in the air, hoping everything would get to where it was supposed to go.

Or is that a myth?

It took everything in me not to take a pregnancy test the next day, but apparently, that's not how these things work. I waited the minimum two weeks (as Google instructed me to).

That fourteenth day, bam—two lines. I took it first thing in the morning, around 6:30 (as Google instructed).

Mike was downstairs making himself lunch to take to work that day, a delicious dish of flavorless chicken and broccoli. I didn't tell him I was taking the test, but I ran downstairs in tears and shoved those two lines right in front of his face.

More tears.

Our entire world was about to change. Every focus shifted. We anxiously went off to work and spent the day texting each other in disbelief, sharing baby names back and forth as if I didn't already have a list in my iPhone notes from two years prior.

For this first pregnancy, we did all the things: the balloons popping out of the box, the baby announcement with our dog in a "big brother" collar, the awkward maternity pictures, the tropical babymoon, and the fully intact nursery by the second trimester that we wouldn't use for another year.

At exactly forty-one weeks, the Eagles played the Saints in the playoffs, and I was in the hospital room being induced. The Eagles lost, but we were about to win the greatest gift of a lifetime. (Too cheesy?)

After a failed induction and almost twenty hours in horrendous back labor, I eventually spiked a fever, and the next thing I knew, I was being prepped for a Cesarean. I threw up incessantly the entire surgery, which looked nothing like the natural and dreamy birth experience that I had fantasized about for forty-one weeks. Expectations: unmet. More of my "planning" shot to hell. I convinced myself this was payback for a relatively easy pregnancy.

Dante came out screaming. Mike cut the cord and brought him over to me. I was still vomiting as I saw my baby for the very first time. As soon as I got stitched up and brought over to the recovery room, the nurse placed my naked baby on my bare chest for the skin-to-skin I was longing for.

Our first son, Dante Joseph DiTore, was born on January 14, 2019, at 4:44 p.m. An absolute dream come true.

We decided we were ready to grow our family again just days after Dante turned one. We found out we were pregnant right before the COVID-19 fiasco began. This made the entire pregnancy and delivery experience much different than our first. This second baby . . . he kept us on our toes the whole pregnancy, which matches his personality now quite well.

We went into our first appointment together after seeing those two pink lines, anxiously expecting to see our baby's heartbeat. But once again, the expectation was unmet. There was no heartbeat. There was a sac but no baby inside it, which meant one of two things:

I was earlier in the pregnancy than I thought.

I had a blighted ovum (the technical term for the growth of a sac but no baby).

All we could do was repeat the ultrasound a week later to see if the baby developed during that time.

One week later, we returned to that ultrasound room, and I stared at that monitor as my heart pounded out of my chest. I cried tears of pure joy when I saw that flicker on the screen. The sac had our new baby, and our new baby had a heartbeat.

A few weeks later, our growing fetus threw us for a loop again when I started bleeding unexpectedly. It was a little bit—and then it was *a lot*. I sat on the toilet in my bedroom, crying my eyes out, wipe after wipe after wipe, hoping that it was all a fluke and the next piece of toilet paper would be clear, as if I was just seeing things that weren't actually there. Every bit of me thought I had lost the baby. In hysterics, I called the nurses' line while I was still sitting on the toilet and was directed to either go to the ER or wait it out for an ultrasound the next morning.

Neither was going to reverse a miscarriage. We chose to wait another day and drove to a distant location for the first available ultrasound appointment. COVID restrictions were put in place by that time, so I attended the ultrasound appointment by myself. I stared at that monitor as my heart pounded out of my chest once again, and I cried tears of joy just as I did the time before. This time, it was more than just a flicker on the screen, though. The sac had a growing baby, and our baby still very much had a heartbeat. A loud, strong heartbeat.

I called Mike before I even walked out of the appointment that day to tell him the good news. Our baby was okay.

* * *

I continued to attend every appointment by myself. I went in for my twenty-week anatomy scan solo, texting Mike as I lay there anxiously waiting to hear good news about our baby's development. I watched that monitor as they moved the cold, gooey wand around my abdomen, trying to figure out the sex as if I had any idea what I was actually looking at.

I felt bad that Mike was missing out on these moments. We feared I'd have to deliver alone, as many women were during the coronavirus pandemic. Fortunately, I did not.

After my first delivery with Dante did not go at *all* as planned (what is a birth plan, anyway?), I was determined to have a

VBAC (vaginal birth after Cesarean) with this second baby. I had a badass midwife whom I'd known from my delivery with Dante. She proved to be an angel on earth. We'll call her "Mo." I don't remember any other nurse or doctor from that day, but she stood out. She was quick and advocated loudly for me in every stage of labor, so I badly wanted her to be a part of my second delivery, too.

During my second pregnancy, Mo gave me motivational talks at each prenatal visit, providing tips and encouragement for a successful VBAC. She'd tell me to put evening primrose up my hoo-ha and to have a lot of sex. Apparently, semen helps soften the cervix. Mike liked Mo.

At thirty-nine weeks, I woke up crampy. I didn't think much of it because going into labor on my own seemed too good to be true. I just assumed this little guy wanted to stay put in there as long as possible, like his big bro. Turns out our second son was ready to party, which also matches his personality today quite well.

As the day went on, the cramps intensified. Like a scene straight out of a movie, I called the nurses' line: "I think I'm having contractions!" I somehow managed to get through the day and put Dante to bed that night in his room. I was in excruciating pain while rocking my first little baby to sleep in his gray rocking chair from Wayfair. Tears streamed down my face as we read *Goodnight Moon* together for his last night as an only child. So much was about to change.

Dante went to sleep, and we quickly threw together a hospital bag (because, hello, second child problems). We went down to the first floor of our townhome, where I wailed on all fours, feeling contraction after contraction as we waited for my mother-in-law to arrive to care for Dante. I threw up the *entire* drive to the hospital. And that . . . that was the last time we ate chicken teriyaki for dinner. It felt like the stars aligned when I saw Mo in the hallway as I was wheeled up to labor and delivery. She looked me dead in the eyes and said, "We're going to have this baby!"

The contractions worsened, and I begged for an epidural. My platelet count was too low, a condition called thrombocytopenia, and I had no luck convincing the doctors that it'd be safe to give me one anyway. This was frustrating, as I am usually quite convincing. Our platelets are responsible for clotting blood, and mine being low put me at a heightened risk for bleeding around my spinal cord with an epidural. My platelet count was always low, but it dropped even lower during each of my pregnancies and even *lower* during my deliveries.

After roughly twenty-four hours in labor and just twenty minutes of pushing (and still *no* epidural), Mo was right—we did it! I was on cloud nine and in pure amazement at what my body had just done. Every push was so powerful. I felt invincible. My son was immediately placed on my chest, and my heart so easily doubled in size. What had I been so worried about? We were meant to be.

Dominic Michael DiTore was born on October 9, 2020, at 8:31 a.m. Another absolute dream.

We went home and witnessed the first moments of a beautiful friendship develop between our two babies. We didn't know at the time how much they'd need each other later on.

We began settling into our life with a toddler and a baby. We had the house, our marriage, two kids, and good jobs. Yes, there was the colic; the chaos; the sleep deprivation; and, of course, the grief for my mom, but most of all, there was an immeasurable amount of love.

I often think about how critical timing played in my sons' conceptions. Had we waited longer to try for a second child, it's very, very likely Dominic wouldn't be here today.

So much good was happening. It was more than I could have ever imagined.

CHAPTER 3

Hey, Google... Can You Save My Husband?

DOMINIC WAS SIX MONTHS OLD, AND DANTE HAD JUST RECENTLY turned two. After being isolated for many months due to the spread of COVID-19, we were so excited to finally get together with family down at the Jersey Shore for the Easter holiday. We had an egg hunt on the beach and woke up to a colorful trail of jelly beans from the Easter bunny leading us from the bedrooms out to the kitchen table. This is the last memory I have from before cancer broke into our lives. It was the last taste of normalcy. But looking back, this trip was also where we saw the first signs of what was to come.

There was a moment in the bedroom that weekend when I handed our youngest son off to Mike, but instead of catching him, he fumbled. Dominic went for a little ride down to the bed, and I shot Mike a look like, "Hello? Pay attention to your child!" (as if he wasn't the world's most attentive and loving father). We didn't think much of it at the time, so we left the shore that weekend and went on with our lives, but these unusual, clumsy moments became more frequent.

Over the next few days and weeks, Mike started losing function in his left hand. He started having difficulty gripping his dumbbells and the pull-up bar in his self-made garage gym. His fingers started sticking to keys as he typed for work. He'd drop cups and spill drinks. He'd walk into things and trip up the steps. Since he was having difficulty lifting weights, he attempted to pick up running, but I vividly remember him coming back from a run with the most defeated look on his face. He told me he had been so uncomfortable because his hand was "flopping around" his whole run.

We went from thinking this was a weight-lifting injury to carpal tunnel syndrome to Lyme disease to finally realizing and accepting that there was something much more severe happening. We started with Mike's primary doctor and an x-ray, which ruled out any physical ailment with his hand. We were then referred to a neurologist. But, of course, we turned to Doctor Google first.

Mike was scared. If you type the symptoms he was having into the search engine, serious illnesses like ALS (amyotrophic lateral sclerosis) are at the top of this list. I was trying so hard to be positive, but inside, I was completely spiraling. Watching Mike experience these neurological symptoms after just recently watching my mom suffer from a neurological disease for many years before succumbing to it in 2019, just three months after Dante was born, sent me down a rabbit hole. I thought, *This can't possibly be happening to us.* It was an uphill battle just trying to schedule an appointment with a neurologist; they were booked for months. But knowing what I know now, I realize every day, week, and month mattered.

After calling several of the neurology practices around, one finally bit. In the time between our primary visit and neurology visit, Mike's symptoms progressed quickly. He had more fatigue and overall balance issues. He was tripping up the steps and becoming very disconnected. He was forced to disengage from our bath and bedtime routine and take a step back from other parenting responsibilities.

It made sense that the neurology office that had availability was the only one that did. The experience was poor, and the doctor was unhelpful. This doctor used electromyography (also known as EMG), a test that detects neuromuscular abnormalities by stimulating a nerve and measuring the muscle's response to that stimulation. The EMG results were normal, and the doctor alleviated our fears of ALS, but she suggested Mike may actually have just been suffering from anxiety. At our request, she handed us a referral for an MRI and said to come back to see her in a month. If she only knew how much our lives would change that next month.

We didn't return to her practice, but I did send a very passionate letter to her and the medical board a few weeks later. This was the very first moment that made me realize that I needed to step up and speak up. We knew in our guts that this was not anxiety, and there was no way I was going to let someone brush off Mike's legitimate feelings—both physical and emotional. I'd be damned if I let a doctor undermine him or try to invalidate what he was experiencing. My mama bear instinct kicked the heck in.

Follow your instincts, people. Speak up.

If we'd listened to this doctor, Mike would probably not have lived another four months.

We had a referral in our hand for an MRI and couldn't get an appointment for weeks (a bigger societal issue we need to deal with, eh?).

As the days went on, Mike began experiencing what he called "brain fog"—a feeling of confusion and fuzziness in his thinking. At that point, he was basically a zombie. A wobbly zombie. Thankfully, we were able to connect with a family friend who works as a radiologist in New Jersey, about an hour and a half from where we lived. His name is Larry. He told us if we left right then, we could get there in time for an MRI that same day.

Mike and I hopped in the car and drove to Larry's facility in Mullica Hill. I sat in the waiting room while Mike went back for the scan.

Afterward, as we waited for that call from Larry, we looked at each other.

"Could that first doctor be right? Could anxiety really be doing this to me?" Mike asked. "Maybe this is all a fluke."

I mean, we sure wanted that to be the case, but in the middle of those hopeful thoughts, my phone rang. It was Larry, prepared to read us the results from the scan Mike had just walked out from.

"Look," Larry said. "This is not a normal MRI." These words are burned into my mind forever. Looking back, I think it was at this very moment that my grief journey began.

Larry told us on that phone call that Mike had a ton of swelling in his brain and multiple lesions. We were instructed to go directly to the emergency room at Inspira Medical Center, a few miles away. For the next week or so, the medical team at Inspira believed that Mike was experiencing some rare kind of demyelinating disease, a condition that damages the layer of protection around each nerve, called the myelin sheath (hence *de-myelinating*). The team thought Mike might have a unique manifestation of multiple sclerosis or possibly a rare vaccination side effect called acute disseminated encephalomyelitis (ADEM)—both of which damage myelin.

However, after a long hospital stay, a spinal tap, several rounds of intravenous steroids, a CT scan, an MRI, and a move to the Jefferson University Hospital system in Philadelphia, where we consulted with a top neurosurgeon, a biopsy was scheduled for just a few days later, on May 21, 2021.

Due to where the lesions were in Mike's brain, they were unable to be safely removed. In fact, there was a risk of creating even more damage to Mike's motor function should a surgeon have tried. Though they couldn't be removed, the medical team was sure they'd be able to at least get a small biopsy of one of the two lesions. This biopsy would both confirm whether these were or were not brain tumors and give the medical team a genetic sample to analyze. The genetic information would tell us if they were cancer and lead us to more targeted treatment options.

During Mike's biopsy, I sat in my in-laws' dining room trying to stomach the chicken bowl we'd just ordered from Panera. My father-in-law was across from me at the other end of the table, and my mother-in-law, sister-in-law, and two young boys were to each of my sides.

Mike was still in the operating room when the surgeon finally called to update me. I stood up and walked into the living room, where everyone could still see me but wouldn't hear the other end of the call.

"The surgery is done, and he's getting stitched up now. Everything went well. We do know that these are gliomas," said the surgeon on the phone.

I immediately asked, "Can you tell if it's cancer?" But that information would take a few more days of testing on the sample they extracted.

If you're familiar at all with brain cancer, you may know that the severity of brain tumors is categorized by "grade" rather than "stage." So, while he confirmed they were gliomas, we didn't know if they were grade one, two, three, or four. The grade predicts its aggressiveness.

A glioma is a tumor made of glial cells that originates in the brain or, sometimes, the spinal cord. According to the Cleveland Clinic, about eighty thousand people are diagnosed with primary brain tumors each year, and 25 percent of them are gliomas.[2] Mike's diagnosis was rare.

Forget all the fancy words and stats for a second. Brain tumors. They were brain tumors. The things I used to convince myself I had every time I had a headache growing up.

I hung up and sat back down at the dining room table with my family.

"They're tumors," I said. But in typical Rebecca fashion, I tried to protect everyone from the news and soften the blow, saying, "They're tumors . . . but they might not even be cancer . . . We were expecting this news anyway. We won't know for a few days if they're cancer, but they could be benign, and he'll get treated, and it'll be fine."

Information is power, but waiting for new information left me with an opportunity to still hope for the least destructive outcome.

Just a few days later, Mike and I were sitting on the couch in our townhome when we received another call from the surgeon who had performed Mike's biopsy. Dante was sitting a few cushions over watching *Sesame Street*, and Dominic was upstairs napping. Mike picked up and put the doctor on speakerphone, and we heard him say something like, "We have most of the genetic analysis back from your biopsy, and it's looking like these are grade three gliomas." Grade three meant cancer. Better than grade four, but not grade one or two.

Cancer. It was brain cancer.

The surgeon followed with, "I don't think we can cure this, but we will treat it . . . and people can live years with this." He said it like it was a "win" for us. Woohoo . . . people *can* live years. But all we took from it was that people also *don't* live years with this.

At that moment, we sank. I remember looking at Mike immediately after hanging up and saying, "It's going to be okay! It's all going to be fine. You have a whole life ahead of you. You *can* live with this!"

Mike didn't want to hear it at the time. To him, he had just been given a death sentence, and I just wanted to protect him from something I really couldn't protect him from. But Lord knows I was going to try. I'd type into Google over and over, "anaplastic astrocytoma success stories" and "grade three glioma prognosis." Various sites on the internet will tell you that someone with this diagnosis will live about three to five years.

I became obsessed with Googling his diagnosis in each and every different way that I could, looking for something good to hang on to. The truth is that the internet has too much information and quite a bit of it is outdated, so much so that I'd start bargaining with everything I read. I'd think, *These statistics include people who are already unhealthy. Who aren't twenty-nine years old. Who don't have a good diet. How many people in this sample exercise like Mike does? Do these stats consider all new technology and clinical trials available?*

But brain cancer doesn't care if you're young and healthy. It doesn't matter if you eat well and exercise daily or if you're a husband and new father or the nicest person on the planet.

It just doesn't give a damn.

CHAPTER 4

No Stone Unturned

I STOOD ON THE BACK DECK OF MY TOWNHOME WITH MY DAD; my oldest brother, Jeff; and my mother-in-law, Debbie. I, as most people would be, was hysterical. The entire life I had planned had just been deconstructed by that surgeon's words.

"I can't live without him," I cried so loudly that I'm sure the connected homes could hear.

"I'm not ready to accept this, either," my brother said back to me.

Was I scared shitless over what a life without Mike would be like? Yes. But I was also numbed by the idea of something happening to *me* now. *What if I get hit by a car tomorrow?* I'd think. *If Mike dies in his early thirties, then there's so much more pressure on me to stay alive. Okay, if I can just stay alive until the kids are, like, twenty-five years old, then they'll be okay without me.* No matter what the internet told me about this diagnosis, I knew I needed to focus on the future and the possibilities rather than potentially old statistics.

Positivity was hard to sustain. It was one punch in the gut after the next. The prognosis wasn't good, especially with the tumors being inoperable, but we were *not* going to let a doctor (or the internet) put a timeline on Mike's life. We were going to do everything in our power to defeat the odds.

I was in denial and then in shock. But I had to snap out of that. I still had babies to wash, butts to wipe, and bellies to fill. So, I put on my invisible cape, declared myself super-mom, and quickly shifted my role from wife to caregiver. I was ready to play superhero and save Mike's life.

I can and I will do it all! I thought. *Just watch!*

It felt as though I was assigned this job of doing the impossible. I believed to my core that I was tasked with saving Mike from an illness that had no cure. But no matter what I could or couldn't do to rescue him from it, I knew I needed to at least pretend to be positive. I needed to have hope. For him. For my kids. For Mike's family. For myself.

I joined Facebook groups and brain cancer communities. I spent hours upon hours in the middle of the night nursing my baby while researching brain cancer treatments and success stories on my phone. Through this, I did develop a true sense of hope. These groups were my saving grace. I found so many stories of people not only living but thriving years and years after diagnosis. One success story alone told me enough to believe that it wasn't *impossible* for Mike to live another decade with this disease.

Again, I'd bargain, *If Mike can survive another ten years, then there will definitely be better treatments available. Maybe even a cure.*

If we can make it another ten years, then the kids will be old enough to have memories of their dad.

From that point, it was game on. Rescue mode: activated.

* * *

Our very first appointment with a neuro-oncologist after Mike's biopsy was virtual. We sat on the first floor of our townhome with my dad on the chair next to us, out of the camera's view. This appointment would tell us more about his diagnosis and next steps. At this point, we were still sort of in shock.

Within that very first conversation, the doctor said to us,

"Do you want to talk *timeline*?"

We both froze, knowing the reality of the disease but not expecting that question. I mean, *already*?

My dad popped in the screen to chime in with, "I don't think that's necessary right now." And thank goodness he did. But I had spent my whole life depending on my dad, and this was another critical juncture point where I realized that I needed to step it up. This was on me, and it was due to our incredible support system that I had the ability to make advocating for Mike my top priority. Mike was depending on me to take care of his needs and speak on his behalf. I needed to come prepared, educated, and ready to question everything at each and every appointment and stand up for my husband, who was too consumed with emotion and his new physical disabilities to understand and process the doctor's jargon. I wasn't going to let the fancy white coat and name tag with half the alphabet on the end intimidate me. *Just try!*

From that point on, I approached every appointment with a new sense of confidence. I initiated every appointment by saying, "We understand the severity of the situation. We need to talk about our options and what *can be done.*"

I stopped doctors in the halls before they walked into his room, and I insisted on a phone call if I couldn't make it to the hospital before they made rounds. I'd make sure Mike was unable to hear me and then say, "Tell your team I do not want anyone walking in there and putting an expiration date on his life. No one is to dare tell him that there's 'nothing they can do'—even if there is nothing they can do!"

I mean, Mike knew. Mike knew the situation he was in, and because he knew, preserving his mental health was key. I tried my best to shelter him from the perpetual stream of bad news.

He didn't need to be kicked further. I wasn't going to let it happen when it was within my control.

I learned first-hand that when you speak assertively and confidently, people are more likely to respect you. I was never rude or demanding; I just did everything I could to talk to his medical team in the most educated way possible. Did I *really* know what I was talking about half the time? Hell no. But I was never going to let anyone talk *at* us.

While our primary neuro-oncologist was at Jefferson University Hospital, we got opinions from doctors all over the world. We consulted with the Mayo Clinic, Fox Chase, and Penn. We connected with a lab in Germany, and we traveled to Duke Cancer Center in North Carolina.

When we road-tripped to Duke, we left our two boys behind with my mother-in-law, Debbie. I sat in the backseat on our eight-hour drive with a blanket over my shoulder, attached to a breast pump. It was hard leaving my baby overnight, but Mike needed me there. When we arrived at his appointment, Mike stood outside of Duke that afternoon and took a picture of the entrance. He posted it to Instagram and wrote, "Leaving no stone unturned." And that's exactly how we approached this disease. Ensuring we left no stone unturned was all we could do to find some amount of peace with what was happening to us.

Mike wasn't believed to have had these tumors since he was a child, but the genetics of the tumor reflected those that were more commonly seen among pediatric patients. Therefore, it was recommended that we add a pediatric oncologist to the team, which is what brought us to Duke in the first place.

The more brilliant minds, the better! Right?

Sort of. Receiving so many opinions was simultaneously comforting and confusing. Part of us wanted each doctor to say the exact same thing. It would have been an easy decision that we'd have felt confident in if every doctor had the same opinion. The other part of us wanted the second-, third-, and fourth-opinion doctors to pull something out of a box that the other doctors didn't know about or have access to. Some doctors recommended we start with "standard of care," which consists of six weeks of radiation with chemotherapy. Some doctors recommended taking a chemotherapy called Temodar *during* radiation, and some recommended taking it *after* radiation. Other doctors recommended an entirely different chemotherapy option. Others recommended just radiation and no chemotherapy. However, no one had much confidence in the success of any of their recommendations.

Standard of care hasn't changed in many years, and that option didn't give us the hope we needed. The doctors were unanimous in saying there was no predicting how the tumors would respond. We understood that, yet still felt puzzled. Why would we start a treatment regimen that was seemingly destined to be unsuccessful?

One tip to anyone reading this book: if you have an inkling of curiosity or confusion about what a doctor is telling you, *ask.* Don't let it go. Don't leave an appointment feeling rushed. Don't let a doctor intimidate you. None of your questions are stupid, and feeling included, educated, and comfortable with the decisions being made regarding treatment could help alleviate any feelings of regret later on. Sometimes, doctors use words that the average person doesn't understand. Request clarification. "Layman's terms, please?" Please . . . speak up. Your peace of mind depends on it.

We didn't feel satisfied with the options we were given and decided to research further, both on our own and with our primary neuro-oncologist at Jefferson. Together, with this doctor's support, we decided to forgo standard of care to pursue a different treatment, as going that standard route seemed pointless.

Our last consultation before making a treatment decision was at Mott Children's Hospital in Michigan. Our doctor at Jefferson had found a clinical trial that would likely be a good fit for Mike. This treatment was designed to target the genetic driver of Mike's tumor. The doctor in Michigan working with this drug described it as "a potential home run."

That's what we needed to hear. *Say no more. We're in.*

As you'll see, it didn't win us the game. But I think the small win we had was part of something much bigger—something potentially life-changing to future brain tumor patients.

We looked back at all we did to get to this treatment option and felt so grateful that we spoke up, got involved, followed our guts, and asked all the questions. We felt a sense of peace knowing that we, again, left no stone unturned.

You know, back at my mom's funeral, my dad shared a story of her in his eulogy. He said that when my brothers were young, the school district they lived in tried to switch the elementary school that our neighborhood was assigned to—the one that my brothers were well-settled into. Everyone in our neighborhood was talking about the change, feeling angry and frustrated. So, our mom—our mama bear—showed up at the next school board meeting, a room packed with unhappy residents, and *she* was the only one who stood up in front of everyone to fight for her babies, to respectfully shut down this obvious disruption to their lives and speak for everyone else who didn't have the fire inside to speak up themselves. She refused to be a doormat, and she spoke up for what she believed in. She asked the questions that were running through everyone's minds.

I'm so damn proud to be that woman's daughter! And I think, just maybe, some of that fire inside her is genetic, as that's how I felt I approached Mike's illness.

As we progressed into Mike's treatment, I also dug deep for resources on how to talk to my children about their daddy's illness—about this obvious disruption to *their* lives.

Speaking to Children About Grief

I consulted several times with a child life specialist, a professional with a background in child development or psychology and experience working with children, who gave me the knowledge and confidence to talk to my kids about what was happening. She was a part of our medical team at Duke, so, at no cost to me, she helped me prepare my kids for what was inevitably going to happen as the illness progressed and, later, ended.

The most memorable piece of information I learned was the importance of being direct and honest with my young boys. It's easy to cutesy up the difficult conversations surrounding death. The overall objective was to let my kids know what was happening without confusing them. Easier said than done, especially when saying "Daddy has cancer" gave me a similar feeling to when I became closely acquainted with our toilet bowl, thanks to the stomach flu, on our last New Year's Eve together. It was physically nauseating.

I instinctively wanted to shelter them from all of it, as if there was some way to hide their daddy's impending death from them. I wanted so badly to preserve their innocence.

Nonetheless, I took the advice I was given. I used the words "cancer," "dying," "tumor," and "death" when it was appropriate.

"I'm taking daddy to the cancer doctor today." "Daddy's brain tumor medicine is making him feel really sick today. He needs extra sleep."

It was an internal battle of trying to normalize something extremely abnormal. However, the goal of being open with them in this way was to encourage them to be open with me in return with their questions and feelings as they came.

Childhood grief is interesting because, at just ages one or two—or even now as I write this book, at ages three and four—my children don't actually know the gravity of what they've lost or what they were losing at the time. They knew something was . . . different. That something really sad was going on. During treatment especially, there were questions and confusion: "Why can't daddy come to the playground with us?" "Is daddy *still* sleeping?"

This specialist provided me with age-appropriate explanations, legacy projects, and books about death, some of which you'll find on my website, linked at the end of this book.

I needed all the guidance I could get.

CHAPTER 5

Home Run

TREATMENT WAS BRUTAL TO MIKE.

He started his six weeks of radiation therapy, but since he could no longer drive, his dad or I drove him forty-five minutes into Philadelphia five days a week for six weeks straight.

We'd pull up to the valet, walk into the building, and ride the elevator down to the basement level. Mike would ring the doorbell outside the radiation room to let them know he was there. He'd put on his custom-made mask and listen to music of his choice (usually hard metal) as the radiation machine targeted its high-energy rays to the precise location of his tumors. Mike would lay there and imagine these rays destroying every last bit of cancer in his brain, attempting to manifest the outcome.

Each treatment would only last about fifteen minutes. His dad or I would hang out in the waiting room until he walked out. We'd go back up the elevator and out to the valet before making the forty-five-minute trek back home, during which we usually listened to the same few Aaron Lewis songs the entire drive.

Radiation in the brain increases swelling around the tumor site, so Mike felt a lot worse before he felt any better. It took so much out of him. His symptoms worsened due to the new swelling, and he could barely keep his eyes open for the next few months.

Since this was over the summer, we tried to spend a couple of days down by the shore together for the Fourth of July. We had family pictures taken in Ocean City, New Jersey, like we did every year, not fully grasping that it could have been the last time. Mike could barely balance on the sand, so we took pictures right outside the house instead of by the ocean like we had in previous years. The left side of his face was numb, so his crooked smile made him dislike almost every picture we took. Those pictures mean everything to me today, though.

That summer, we also coordinated a time for his best friend, Rocky, to surprise Mike by proposing to his now wife right at my family's beach house. Nobody knew what the next week, month, or year would look like, and Rocky wanted Mike to be a part of it. I set up a blanket outside the house with flowers and a bottle of champagne. It was raining, and the blanket became soaking wet, but we weren't going to allow it to ruin the moment.

Rocky texted me when he arrived at the house, and I took Mike down the elevator in our house from the second floor to the garage. A lot of houses down by the shore are now built with elevators, and we are so fortunate to have one of them, as it came in handy with both my mom's and Mike's disabilities.

My anxiety to execute this moment and give Mike this special surprise was high. But as we were headed downstairs to meet them, we got stuck in the elevator for at least fifteen minutes. I was banging on the door, screaming up to my family on the second floor while Rocky was behind the house in the pouring rain, nervously trying to buy time and acting like the romantic little setup in our backyard had nothing to do with their visit. It was as if Rocky's future was in the hands of this crappy little home elevator. Meanwhile, Mike had no idea what was going on or why I was so worked up.

We eventually made it downstairs, and when Mike saw Rocky in the backyard, he was as surprised as I could have ever hoped for. It's as if he had a rush of energy that I hadn't seen in him for many months. We laughed, we hugged, we talked, and then we shared their beautiful proposal moment before popping some champagne to celebrate. I know this meant the world to Mike and even more to Rocky, as Mike never did make it to his wedding, which took place just days before he died.

* * *

After six gruesome weeks of radiation, Mike started the experimental treatment, called avapritinib, as well as an intense physical and occupational therapy regimen. With the combination of these therapies and the improvements from radiation, Mike regained so much strength.

We crammed a lot into those next few healthy months. We moved into a new home shortly after he finished radiation, a home right down the street from his family, knowing we'd need more hands-on support moving forward. It was a home we thought, at the time, would be our "forever" home.

We celebrated Dominic's first birthday with a pumpkin-themed party at a local park, surrounded by friends and family.

Mike was back in the gym, lifting weights five days a week. He returned to work by the end of 2021, and his boss said it was as if he had never left at all. He went hunting in Potter County, Pennsylvania, with his dad over the holidays, something that he looked forward to every single year. He wasn't sure if he should go but had an inkling that it would be his last opportunity. He didn't come home with a buck, but he did come home with special memories and a positive COVID test.

Mike got his long-awaited tattoos during this time—a half sleeve with four lions representing us and our two boys, as well as an "R" on his ring finger. His weight fluctuated so much throughout his treatment that his wedding ring didn't fit any longer.

We took a family trip to Disney World, with the unspoken understanding that it could very likely be the only one we'd have with all four of us together.

And I threw Mike a thirtieth birthday party in our new home. Friends we hadn't seen in years showed up and surprised him at our front door. While we had fun, it was hard to suppress the nagging reminder that it might just be the last time we celebrated his birthday here on earth.

Through it all, we saw significant improvements in Mike's health, but the medication caused terrible side effects. He lost and gained weight, felt extremely fatigued, and experienced stomach complications almost daily. He powered through as much as he could every single day.

We requested Mike's January MRI be moved up to take place right before our trip to Disney, hoping we could enjoy our trip knowing things were going well.

In my online patient and caregiver communities, I learned of the term "scanxiety." Scanxiety is the stress and worry you feel while awaiting the next round of imaging during cancer treatment.

Mike was scheduled to get an MRI every three months indefinitely. The scans were scheduled out a few weeks in advance, so in those few weeks leading up to each one, the scanxiety would start to creep in. I'd become hyper-focused on Mike's every move and start questioning him on how he was feeling. *Most* of the time, the scan would reflect how Mike was doing physically. His two post-treatment scans up to that point had reflected the significant strides he had made over those few months. Nonetheless, we'd worry. As we approached his scan date, our thoughts would become more intrusive, and sleeping at all on the eve of the scan was impossible. Thankfully, our neuro-oncologist would call us the day after the scan to give us a quick "Everything looks good!" or "The scan is stable— no new spots!" This alleviated some of the post-scan anxiety, since the full report would typically take a few days.

We received news after that MRI on January 13, 2022, that we didn't even think was possible. The medication sure seemed like the "home run" we were hoping for. His tumors were virtually undetectable. One doctor commented that it looked like Mike's *inoperable* tumors were completely removed by surgery. It was truly a miracle, and our medical team said the level of improvement they saw in his scans was extremely rare. We all had so much hope—hope that Mike would well out-live that internet prognosis and hope that we may just have more of that future together that we imagined.

However, it often felt like when things were going really well, whether it was just a few days of no nausea or a really good scan, there was always something else unwanted taking shape simultaneously. There was always some little reminder, as if to say, *don't get too comfortable here.*

Just a few days after that news, we got a call from the doctor telling us that Mike would need to hold off on taking his medication until his white blood cell count increased. It had been steadily dropping throughout the month and had just officially fallen below the allowed parameters for his medication. A low white blood cell count increased Mike's risk for infection, which could have taken his life before cancer did. This was a huge blow after *just* getting the reassurance that this drug was doing what we hoped it would.

Mike stopped taking the medication briefly, but after more evaluation, the team decided to continue with a lower dose while collecting weekly labs and administering a blood marrow stimulant in the form of an injection.

We'll be back on track soon enough, we convinced ourselves.

CHAPTER 6

If You're Not Laughing, You're Crying

AFTER TAKING A BREAK FROM HIS TUMOR MEDICATION FOR only a week during the white blood cell mishap, the side effects were strangely very different once Mike returned to the lower daily dose. It felt as if he had started an entirely different medication, and we couldn't understand why.

The previous nausea and diarrhea that Mike had sadly become accustomed to turned into incessant vomiting, perhaps exacerbated by the new injection that we added to the regimen. Mike couldn't keep any food, medication, or liquids down for days. He was back on his medication, but his body really wasn't absorbing it. We became increasingly concerned about dehydration and, of course, why this was happening in the first place. Why would his body be rejecting this medication? It was supposed to save his life.

After a few days of vomiting, we drove to the ER closest to our home in hopes of getting him some immediate relief and (wishful thinking) a same-day MRI. We got the first accomplished. Mike was given fluids and Zofran through an IV, a more effective and fast-acting method than taking it orally, which he already did daily. Unfortunately, the hospital staff couldn't schedule him for an MRI that day, so once he began feeling better from the IV, he came home. His next MRI had already been moved up a few weeks due to this sudden change in symptoms, but waiting even just two more days felt like waiting a lifetime.

After returning home from that visit, the Zofran wore off yet again, and the nausea and vomiting returned with a vengeance. Mike spent most of his days back and forth between the bathroom and our bed, trying to just survive until his next MRI. There was hardly an opportunity to feel the scanxiety.

On scan day, we woke up together in our bed. I got up first to grab our boys and take them down for breakfast as we waited for my mother-in-law to arrive to watch them while I drove Mike to his scan. Mike was slowly making his way out of bed and into the bathroom to get ready.

About a half hour later, Mike called me back upstairs.

"Bec?" he yelled.

I walked into the room, and from our bed, Mike asked, "What happened?" He said, "I was in the bathroom, and I don't know what happened."

I was confused. I got in the bed next to him, and it didn't take long to realize that something was very wrong. He didn't know the time, day, or place. He was struggling to speak at all. My gut told me that during the time that I was getting the boys up and fed, he had his very first seizure in the bathroom because he was dehydrated and had been vomiting up his anti-seizure medication. My mother-in-law walked in at the exact same time that I was coming back down the stairs to get my phone and call for medical help.

I called 911, and Mike and I took our first ambulance ride over to the hospital—not a "first" together worth celebrating. I sat in the front seat of that ambulance in so much fear. I called Mike's doctor on the way there to let her know what had happened.

Obviously, at that moment, my concern was Mike. However, the thought of our three-year-old son witnessing me run back downstairs in tears to call 911 left me with unbearable knots in my stomach—on top of the ones created by this situation to begin with.

I couldn't help but wonder what impact all this was having on him. *How much does he understand?* I thought.

I knew children comprehend more than we think, and I never wanted them to feel worried or unsafe. It had appeared as though they felt my panic that morning. Thankfully, Dante and Dominic were having a blast at home. They seemed to move on from the moment, despite it sticking with me all day long.

We arrived at the ER in the ambulance, and the testing quickly began. Mike spent four days in the hospital while getting just about every test available once again—CT scan, MRI, short and long EEGs, another MRI, and various labs. The MRI took a few attempts over the course of his stay because, in his condition, he couldn't follow commands or stay still long enough for the test to be done correctly. He was agitated and confused, unable to understand me or the hospital staff and unable to communicate himself. What he wanted to say simply did not match the words that were coming out of his mouth. He was in such distress that the medical team caring for him actually insisted on shackling him down until he could relax because he was pulling the EEG tape off his head. He didn't know what was going on, but to me, it was incredibly disturbing to watch.

Mike was given sedatives, but he fought them with every bit of energy he had, which complicated things more. Those first two days in the hospital were terrifying. Nobody knew why Mike was acting the way that he was. We originally thought he was facing extreme dehydration, but after hours of getting pumped with fluids and no improvement, we knew it was something more. The following were the possibilities at that point:

- ongoing mini seizures
- tumor growth
- stroke
- infection
- medication toxicity

Of course, tumor growth and stroke were our biggest concerns—both of which, after more evaluation, were ruled out. In fact, his MRI looked the same as the month prior—virtually no active cancer.

Infection was ruled out next, and an EEG showed no present seizure activity. This isn't to say that he didn't experience one at home; in fact, it's assumed that he probably did. The "theory" was that there was actually some combination of these things at play. We think Mike had a reaction to the infusion of his new medication that he received to prevent infections, which worsened his already present nausea. The exacerbated nausea and vomiting then led to severe dehydration and a lack of medication absorption—meaning his body was not absorbing the anti-seizure medication that he took daily, as we predicted. All of this, we believe, led to a seizure and explained his altered mental state.

In an "injured" brain, seizure recovery can take a lot longer than it might in a healthy brain. After a couple of days in the hospital, Mike finally woke up seeming much more like himself.

I was constantly going back and forth from the hospital to my house over those few days. There were times that I left late at night and other times when I stayed overnight in an uncomfortable hospital chair by Mike's side. Sometimes, I'd even squeeze into the bed next to him. The last night he was at the hospital, I knew he was on the mend, so I left a little early to be home with the kids while his dad stayed by the foot of the bed. Mike called me the next morning, and my heart literally exploded out of my chest. I was so damn happy to not only hear his voice but to hear him stringing words together and actually making sense. There was a period of time during the hospital visit that I thought he may have permanently lost his cognition.

Outside of some short-term memory loss and dysfunction using his phone, the change overnight was remarkable. The next day, even better.

Despite how scary it had been, we were able to laugh at some of the things he said while coming out of this funk, like when he professed his unwavering love for pizza and when he told the doctor our boys' names were "Dominic and Bominic." Sometimes, in these situations, if you're not laughing, you're crying. We did a lot of both.

Mike was eventually discharged with a new medication and some better strategies for nausea management. We started using a Sancuso patch for the very first time, which I replaced on Mike's arm every six to seven days, and it proved to be very helpful in managing his nausea over the following months.

We left the hospital that day with renewed hope (once again), but only for so long.

Remember, DiTores, don't get too comfortable!

CHAPTER 7

"What Have I Become..."

JUST AS WE STARTED TO CELEBRATE MIKE'S ONE-YEAR SURVIVAL mark, the universe told us to check ourselves.

We'd had one whole year of doctor appointments, travel, treatments, pills, nausea, fatigue, weight gain, weight loss, infusions, injections, hospitalizations, MRIs, tears, and celebrations—it felt like we'd come such a long way. We had so much hope. The progress Mike had made was a result of hard work and dedication. We were finally beginning to get a handle on this "new normal" when it was so quickly ripped out from under us *again*. We learned a lot that year, but especially that brain cancer is a cruel and unpredictable m'fer.

Ever since our hospital debacle earlier in the year, Mike had something called nystagmus, which, according to the American Academy of Ophthalmology, is a condition with which the eyes move rapidly and involuntarily.[3] He couldn't move his eyes all the way to the right or left, and when he tried, his eyes would wiggle uncontrollably. Besides possible tumor growth, there was really no explanation for it. Since his tumor in the last MRI at the hospital still appeared stable, it was chalked up to a delayed effect from radiation.

This was an extremely frustrating ailment that Mike never complained about. It lasted for several weeks, until one Saturday afternoon when we took our older son to his soccer practice. I was on the turf with our two boys while Mike was in the bleachers watching. At some point, in the middle of the game,

Mike's side-eye wiggle turned into full-blown double vision in an instant.

When it was time to leave, I walked over to him on the bleachers and watched him almost fall on his face. He couldn't stand up straight. I held onto him and our kids as we walked to the car together.

Though Mike was constantly filled with fear and frustration, the car ride home was the very first time he actually let it out toward the kids and me. After buckling the kids in their car seats, I sat down and dialed the off-hours line for his doctor. I should have put this number first on my "favorites" list because I called them constantly. As the phone rang, Dante asked for something (and, in good old toddler fashion, repeated his request over and over and over). Mike turned around and, in obvious frustration, shushed him loudly.

I was ultra-sensitive to how we spoke to the kids. I didn't want them to necessarily feel the insane amount of emotion that we were feeling. They were already going through a lot, so when anyone had less than *a lot* of patience for them, I got extremely defensive. I immediately scolded Mike for overreacting to Dante's request, but as a result, I overreacted to Mike. I mean, 99.9 percent of the time, he handled every situation with patience and grace despite the absolute explosion waiting to happen inside of him. I can't imagine trying to walk around for one hour with double vision, let alone for weeks or months.

Just hours after that soccer practice, we went to get another scan at Abington Memorial Hospital, the local hospital we frequented. We went to the ER in hopes of getting expedited testing that we'd otherwise have to wait days for. And we did. I remember that at each ER visit, we'd first get the CT scan results, and each and every time they were normal, I'd have a sense of relief as we waited for the MRI results next. But this time, the MRI results took forever.

There we were—Mike lying in the hospital bed, unable to see a clear picture, and me, unable to sit down for a second, walking back and forth, fidgeting, and asking the nurse every five minutes for an update.

We waited and waited.

As I anxiously paced back and forth in the hospital hallway, I turned around and saw Mike taking a video of me to the song "Patience" by Guns N' Roses, singing along for me to take it slow and have a little patience. In the midst of my internal crisis, just waiting to get Mike's new, expedited death sentence from the doctor, I busted out in laughter. That was the thing about Mike. No matter how difficult things were for him, he was always looking out for me. He was always the calm to my storm—my anchor, as my therapist referred to him.

"We just have to wait," he'd tell me. And we did wait. Far too long.

We were eventually told the radiology team had left for the night, and we wouldn't get his results until the following day. A few gray hairs later, we survived the wait and left the hospital visit the next day with a stable MRI report and an appointment with a neuro-ophthalmologist to get a prescription for prism glasses. Honestly, I never even knew such a specialty existed!

Until that visit, Mike wore an eye patch or glasses to which I had taped black construction paper over the left lens. Covering one eye still left him with blurred vision, but it relieved the double vision. When he wasn't cracking pirate jokes at himself, he was wobbling around the house singing "Hurt" by Johnny Cash, asking what he had become as a result of all his problems.

Everyone handles things differently, but people would often

ask me, "How did you do it?" How did I watch my husband lose everything that made him *him*? How did I watch him wrap his head around his impending mortality? How did I endure the physical and emotional strains of a caregiver? How did I mother (well) through it all?

I did it with a lot of patience, a commitment to hope, and an unwavering love. I did it by never seeing *not* doing it as an option. I didn't want any of this to happen, but taking care of him was what I vowed to do. It's one of the things I was called on this earth to do. Physically, I did it with a lot of help from family members, nurses, and aids. Mentally, though? I did it with a combination of humor and music.

Mike would take every opportunity to lighten the moment and make me laugh. I was on the floor belly laughing when he used to pretend to be cartel boss Hector Salamanca from *Breaking Bad* and act as if he was angrily ringing a bell on the arm of his wheelchair when he needed something. He did as much for me as I did for him on those really difficult days. Those small moments of happiness were everything to us.

Not everyone will shed the positivity that Mike did while dealing with a terminal illness. Hell, if I was in Mike's position, I don't think I would have been able to handle it that way. The reality is that we can't predict how we'd navigate that situation until we're in it. Mike was living through an unfathomable level of suffering, both physically and emotionally, and I think anyone in that situation gets a pass to cope in whatever way they need to.

I remember when we were referred to a neurologist for the first time, Mike looked at me and said, "I just don't want it to be my brain; things with your brain change who you are." Because in many cases, the location of a brain tumor can directly affect a patient's personality and ability to regulate emotions.

In fact, I've connected with other widows who've told me that before they ever found out about their husbands' brain cancer diagnoses, they were actually considering divorce, as they couldn't understand why their loving spouses were suddenly so angry and irritated toward them. Those people didn't really have a choice in how "positive" they were.

We felt a combination of relief for a seemingly stable MRI and frustration that there was no solution for Mike's double vision. An eye patch and prism glasses felt more like slapping a Band-Aid on than actually making him better.

The thing was, there was no getting better.

The prism glasses provided some relief for about forty-eight hours but quickly became of no use. They were prescribed based on Mike's needs on the very day we met with the ophthalmologist, but his vision was changing and worsening every single day.

A few weeks later, around Easter 2022, just one year after his symptoms first appeared, things took a huge turn for the worse. We managed to get through Easter morning with the kids (another jelly bean trail to the kitchen table), but Mike was in really bad shape the whole day.

He began struggling with just about every normal function—his vision worsened, he lost hearing in his left ear, his speech and ability to swallow became more affected, and his overall balance and coordination became so impaired that he needed full assistance getting around.

I couldn't even begin to understand the sadness and frustration Mike was feeling. He'd lost so much independence in such a short amount of time. No matter how much I helped him, I felt so completely helpless, and watching him struggle was *hard*.

After more time spent in the hospital, an MRI revealed new tumor growth in a different location than last time. It was found in an extremely critical part of his brain—a location too dangerous to operate on (yet again), or to even biospy. It was assumed to be as aggressive, if not more aggressive, than his first diagnosis, but time was the only way to tell.

We were expecting bad news, given all of Mike's quickly developing symptoms, but we were somehow still in shock. We always knew a recurrence was possible—even quite likely—down the road, but we certainly didn't anticipate it happening that soon. We never ignored changes in Mike's symptoms, and we were always quick to call the doctor at any hour. We visited the ER on multiple occasions to expedite imaging and other testing when something concerned us. We couldn't wrap our heads around it. We had done everything "right." It felt like the universe kept knocking us down every time we saw a glimpse of light. *Hey, DiTores, once again, don't forget! No comfort allowed!*

This new diagnosis felt like an entirely new trauma. We knew his treatment options would be limited this time around, given how soon he'd need radiation. A recurrence so soon, just one year later, didn't bode well for the overall prognosis.

To be blunt, I knew this was the beginning of the end. I knew as soon as I heard this new diagnosis that we were down to just months together. Maybe I wasn't ready to accept it yet. But deep down, I knew . . .

For a while, I wondered, *why us?* And when I stopped wondering that, I started wondering, *Why right now? Why when our babies are so young?* I struggled to believe there was some grander plan the universe had for us at Mike's expense. We were back to square one and felt an overpowering sense of defeat—as if every single effort we had put in over the last year meant *nothing.*

CHAPTER 8

In Sickness and in Health

When the doctors looked back to compare his post-Easter MRI to the one he'd had back in February, aided by all the new symptom information, they could actually identify very small changes in Mike's brain stem. This time, the tumor wasn't a mass; it was a diffuse infiltrating glioma. This meant that the tumor was growing throughout his brain stem and intertwining with regular brain tissue. The brain stem is an extremely critical part of our brains and is responsible for almost every involuntary function needed to survive, including blood pressure, heart rate, and breathing patterns. According to the National Institutes of Health, the brain stem connects the cerebrum of the brain to the spinal cord and cerebellum.[4] Growth in this part of his brain explained the episodes of increased heart rate he started experiencing after his recurrence that we originally thought were due to panic attacks.

The brain stem is small, so there didn't have to be *a lot* of tumor to do *a lot* of damage. There were also signs of leptomeningeal disease, which is when cancer spreads to the cerebrospinal fluid. I knew the word "leptomeningeal" from my earlier research and was familiar with the prognosis being only a couple of months. After hearing this news, I lay in the hospital bed with Mike, and he gave me the most heartfelt apology.

As if, somehow, this was his fault.

The treatment would be three weeks of radiation followed by a different chemotherapy, which required him to stop the other medication he'd been taking from Michigan. This new growth was the most pressing.

It all felt different this time. I felt helpless and was desperate to find reasons to be hopeful. I think these two entries from the blog I started during Mike's illness depict my true feelings from that time:

> **Journal Entry from May 4, 2022:**
> *I'll never know why this is happening. I'll never know why we have to go through such pain, but there are so many things that I hope can come out of this . . .*
> *I hope that we're the family sharing our story of defeating the odds and coming out stronger despite every card being stacked against us. I hope we're the family able to provide hope to others going through a similar situation.*
>
> *I hope that by facing such adversity so early in life, Dante and Dominic grow up to be empathetic, compassionate, and resilient human beings. I hope they spread only kindness in the world. I hope they treat others with dignity and respect. I hope they understand the importance of their words and know that anyone they come in contact with could have a heart that's hurting.*
>
> *I hope that by witnessing how we're taking care of daddy, our boys see not only the importance of helping others but an example of unconditional love. I often think about how much they're absorbing from the way I interact with Mike and respond to his*

needs. That very thought guides my every move. That thought grounds me in my moments of frustration. We stood at the altar at twenty-five years old, reciting every word the priest said. In sickness and in health. We were young and could have never prepared for the weight those words would hold so soon after. I'd recite those very same vows one hundred times over, and I hope that our love for each other positively influences our children's future relationships.

I hope our boys know that they are inherently strong but that they don't always have to be. In those moments of weakness, I hope they know that it's okay to show emotion and to get help when things feel unmanageable—that it's okay to talk about feelings. I hope they know that asking for help shows their very strength, and by doing so, they can and will get through life's hardships.

I hope our boys learn that family always shows up. Our families are one team with the very same goals: to make sure they feel secure and loved immeasurably while maintaining as much normalcy for them as possible and to make sure Mike has the absolute best care and every opportunity to fight this . . .

Their grandparents and I are the best team I've ever been a part of. Aunts and uncles and great-aunts and uncles make a point of visiting and lending a hand. Great mom-mom, at ninety-four years old, makes homemade pasta for Mike every week, since it's one of the few things he can comfortably eat right now. Friends and even acquaintances have sent activities for the boys, meals, gift cards, and support.

I hope we all learn to be grateful and present in moments that seem small or insignificant. To stop scrolling and put down the phone. When you're battling cancer or loving someone who is, you are forced to live day by day, even hour by hour, and those seemingly small moments are, in fact, big moments.

As for Mike, today, he completed his first of fifteen radiation treatments on this new growth in his brain stem. We're in for a really challenging few weeks, as radiation typically makes everything much worse before there's any improvement. Over the next week, I'll be working with our doctors to devise a plan for after these treatments are done. Now that we're dealing with this metastasis in the brain, we're in a more difficult situation. Our doctor at Michigan is always willing to think outside the box, and our doctor at Jefferson is always willing to support our plan. We went for another opinion last week at another local university, and the doctor was pessimistic and unproductive. He told us it would be nearly impossible to find a clinical trial should we go that route. We're writing him off as quickly as he did us.

At the very least, he left us more confident in the medical team we already have in place. There is no sure-shot treatment for this. Then again, there wasn't one the first time either—but where there is life and there are options, there is hope.

Journal Entry from May 26, 2022:
Mike finished his fifteenth and final radiation treatment this week. Finishing radiation feels different this

time around. It's not because I'm any less proud of him and his perseverance. It's not because it's any less of an accomplishment, either. Watching Mike ring that bell and hearing the applause from the staff that has become so invested in him is special. It's emotional. It's all just different this time. Last summer, after six weeks, Mike rang that bell, and it felt like a huge celebration. We knew this battle wasn't over. We know it never will be, but we thought we were closing the chapter on it for some meaningful amount of time. I don't even know how much time. A few years, maybe? Finishing radiation last year meant Mike was on the road to recovery. He was on the path back to being the amazing, involved, hands-on husband and daddy that he was meant to be.

That being said, I have come to really dislike the saying "Everything happens for a reason." And "What's meant to be will be." It feels like a load of BS. Mike is meant to be digging in the dirt out back with our boys; he's meant to be running around with us at the park and coming for walks with us around the neighborhood. He's meant to be reading books and singing songs with us at bedtime. We're meant to be doing things together. We're meant to be getting out of the house for date nights . . . not only for doctor's appointments. These things were meant to be, but cancer came in with no regard to begin writing its own version of our story. That new story might be our reality right now, but it is not the story that was ever meant to be. I just very recently saw an Instagram post about the unfairness of life that author Zero Dean *writes about in his book. Part of the excerpt was about being a warrior and working through whatever life throws your way with courage, love, and positivity, and continuously pushing forward. Because you're a survivor of the unfairness of life.[5]*

I do feel like we're being unfairly robbed of so much, but I'm really trying to stay strong and manifest the mindset that this quote encourages.

Anyway, this time around, radiation felt different because it means the disease has progressed. It means we're now facing a much steeper mountain. It means that since ringing that bell again, we've entered back into this black hole of the unknown. I am not hopeless, but having done everything "right" the first time around and still ending up here again so soon inevitably leaves me more intimidated.

It's hard to explain the extent of the damage this new tumor has done. Mike is just not Mike right now. He's extremely worn down, and radiation was hard. He is struggling with his new disabilities and new level of dependence on us. While there have been some minor improvements (such as in his ability to balance on all fours), he's also regressed in other areas, such as communication. While he was once able to disconnect from this reality a little bit through back and forth with friends or on social media, he now struggles to use his phone. We are forced to have patience and take things no faster than moment by moment. It's been the challenge of a lifetime, but the support we've received over the last few weeks has been incredibly heartwarming. We had no idea how many people were so invested in

our story and so badly rooting for our family.
Next step is an MRI in three weeks . . .

* * *

Mike still worked through physical, occupational, and speech therapy almost daily. If the therapists weren't over, then I'd take him through each exercise on our family room floor myself. I'd help him move from the couch to the floor, and we'd work on movements that used to be a part of his post-workout stretch but were now extremely challenging exercises for him.

This man who used to squat more than I weighed now struggled to simply lift his arms over his head. We took videos sometimes in hopes of seeing improvement over time, just like after his initial diagnosis. But he continued to struggle—more and more every day. These videos now serve as a reminder of the unbearable heartbreak we felt as we simultaneously began seeing for ourselves that there was no getting better. Despite a bit of denial, we were in the midst of accepting defeat. Eventually, with his lack of progress, it made no sense for occupational and physical therapists to continue coming.

Nurses were also over every day to check Mike's vitals and bed sores. He was connected to an IV at home for fluids at least three times a week to keep him hydrated. The hydration helped his nausea. He was taking over fifteen pills a day for nausea, anxiety, seizures, and pain.

My mother-in-law was over every single morning by 7 a.m. to help me get everyone dressed and downstairs for the day. We'd call ourselves the "dream team" as we worked together every minute of the day to meet the needs of Mike, Dante, and Dominic in a way that allowed everyone to get attention and stay comfortable at home.

Thankfully, my kids were young, and they became used to our caregiving routine. They were used to the medical equipment all over our house—the upstairs wheelchair and the downstairs wheelchair, the commode, the chairlift, and the big ramp in our garage. When I think about all the hands and equipment we needed to get through those days, it solidifies that caregiving is *no joke.* I'd seen it done, but it isn't until *you* are the one that you really understand what it takes. The lifting and readjusting. The bathing and toileting and feeding. The intense pressure to do it all with a smile—even when you're drowning. There is a strenuous amount of time, effort, and patience involved.

That being said, I never looked at my caretaking responsibilities as a bother or burden, so I sure as hell didn't want Mike to feel that he was either of those things. Of course, when three people are asking things of you every minute of the day, there are moments of frustration. I am only human. But caring for him was the honor of my life.

In fact, looking back at all those times that Mike tried to make me smile in the hospital room made me even more cognizant of the moments I had available to do the same for him. Each day, I'd lift him out of his wheelchair and into the chair lift. Before I held the button down to send him up to the staircase landing where I would transfer him onto the second half of the lift, I'd ask him what he wanted me to sing to him. Sometimes, he'd smile and pick a song. Other times, I'd default to "What's Your Fantasy" by Ludacris or "Cleanin' Out My Closet" by Eminem. We'd both chuckle as we rapped our way upstairs together.

As I've mentioned, I had tremendous support each day. My mother-in-law helped me take care of everyone, and my dad came over every single afternoon around 4 p.m. to occupy the boys so Mike could have my undivided attention. He stayed to help the boys get washed, brushed, and ready for bed while I helped Mike get washed, brushed, and ready for bed. My father-in-law stayed over every single night after he got done working because Mike and the boys both had middle-of-the-night needs, and there was only one of me.

In the thick of caregiving, it was when Mike and the kids were finally asleep that I had a minute to catch my breath, but I didn't always want to. I didn't necessarily want peace and quiet. The quiet bred loneliness. I felt it even when surrounded by others, too, though. It was lonely being the only one who understood where I was in my grief. Anticipatory grief hits you at all stages of illness. I couldn't understand how people were still going about their lives. It felt so weird to me that friends were going out to dinner and still living—but they needed to. Mike would never have wanted anything else. I'd walk around the grocery store feeling like people were staring and talking. "She's the one whose husband is dying . . ."

But at the same time, I felt invisible. None of the strangers walking the produce aisle had a damn clue about my life. I wanted to scream to every single person I ran into, "How don't you know?!"

Since we knew that the MRIs usually aligned with how Mike was doing physically, his follow-up MRI was what we suspected. Worse, actually. He had several new spots on his brain, and the one that had just been radiated had grown bigger through treatment.

Journal Entry from June 29, 2022:

As many of you know, instead of finding the relief we were expecting and hoping for from radiation, Mike's health has continued to go downhill. Watching him struggle is a pain I can't explain. I'm filling out preschool paperwork for my son and palliative care paperwork for my husband. I'm reading books to my kids about death and grief. There is nothing natural about any of this. I always say this, but it really does feel like I'm telling someone else's story.

It is an absolute privilege to be the one these three boys depend on for comfort. For direction. For survival. It's a rewarding and purposeful job, but it's also heavy. I fear every single day for my boys should something happen to me. You get married, have kids, and have a will drawn up because it's what you're supposed to do to be a responsible parent. We were twenty-six years old and in full-blown baby mode. We knew the importance of the decisions we were making, but we were also checking items off the pregnancy "to-do list." This whole situation opens your eyes to the fact that bad things can literally happen to anyone at any time. It's horrible, and it's unfair, but it's true.

I think in my role as caregiver, I've put this impossible pressure and responsibility on myself to save Mike. I really believed I had a chance at saving him from this monster that is brain cancer. I wanted to believe that I had more control. It feels like there is so much more to try, but the rate at which things are changing is limiting us. We are in what feels like an impossible situation with a tumor growing in a pattern that excludes us from every clinical trial and growing in a location that cannot be biopsied. Without the biopsy, we can't learn the genetic information needed to ac-

cess a targeted treatment like we did the first time. The tumor is extending into the most critical parts of his brain. He took a dose of chemotherapy a few weeks ago to help slow things down, but more time will never be enough.

The physical exertion of a caregiver is difficult, but it's the mental overload that really challenges me. It's the anxiety over what life is going to look like one week, one month, one year from now. It's the indescribable fear of Dante and Dominic's future and the pain they will inevitably feel throughout. It's the bills that need to be paid, the support accessories that Mike needs, the tracking of medications and appointments, and the daily messaging with the nursing team. It's the scheduling of physical therapy, speech therapy, occupational therapy, nursing, wound care, and fluids. It's remembering what food staples we're out of because if we go one day without applesauce or waffles, the boys might chop my arm off. It's the constant thought, What more could I be doing? It's dealing with long-term disability claims and COBRA. It's the guilt of wondering if all of these administrative tasks are taking too much quality time away from Mike and the boys. Do I have a choice? Did I spend enough one-on-one time with everyone today? It's moving quickly when Mike has new symptoms that need immediate attention at any hour. It's the self-control it takes to stay calm when Mike's in distress but my kids are hanging on my shirt, asking me to stop and come play. It's striving to limit screen time but also finding myself in those moments of desperation. It's the middle-of-the-night needs and lack of *sleep. It's trying to find the time and resources to help myself process this better.*

I feel so much sadness, but I'm also realizing how little of this whole situation I am actually processing. Things are moving too fast, and my mind can't keep up. I do have so much help at home. I could never, ever diminish the level of dependency I have on my dad and my in-laws. I need them. We all do. Nobody would get the level of care and attention they get now if it wasn't for our family stepping in all day, every day.

I've been following a woman named Nora McInerny—an author and podcast host. Nora's husband died from brain cancer when her son was two years old. I first listened to her TED Talk years ago about grief around the time that my mom died. There are so many feelings that come up throughout this journey, and it feels like a process that so few can relate to. Grief is different for everyone. The experience is different for each person, even when grieving the very same person. There are so many things I've read and heard in Nora's work that make me feel so validated in what I've been feeling over the past thirteen months.

In one of her podcast interviews, she and her guest talk about how grief actually begins at diagnosis. I never thought about it like that—but it's absolutely true. I am grateful to still hold Mike's hand and tell him I love him today, but I realized that I have been grieving since his diagnosis last May. The moment we heard "brain cancer" was the moment my head and heart started feeling the pull between being extremely hopeful and also realizing that life will never be the same. *Despite our optimism, the life we imagined to-gether died in that moment. Since Mike's diagnosis, I've been grieving the partnership and companion-ship this illness robbed us of. I've been grieving for our boys and the childhood we envisioned for them. I've been grieving our entire family dynamic. I've been grieving family dinners together at the table—just the four of us. I've been grieving the idea of us ever becoming a family of five. I've been grieving my very own identity while learning my new role as caregiv-er—which I take on with absolute honor but wouldn't wish on anyone at thirty years old or ever.*

For the last thirteen months, I've tried to fully be-lieve that we will defy all odds and have many, many years ahead of us, but it would be unrealistic for me not to simultaneously consider the alternative. I am trying to wrap my head around how I will possibly move forward as our world comes crashing in. I will never lose all hope—but the emotions that come along with this are so complex.

As for the bros . . . Each night, I lie in bed with Dan-te until he falls asleep. We read a book or two, say a prayer, chitchat, cuddle, and a few minutes later, he's out. We each say a few things that we're thankful for. Dominic is a firecracker every single waking second. His sheer will to do absolutely anything he shouldn't be doing, all with a big smile on his face, keeps us on our toes and laughing throughout the days. He's too young to have an emotional connection to this, but he has an incredibly sweet heart. When he's not climbing tables or playing with dog food, he sits with Mike. He pushes the wheelchair and pretends he's helping us transfer him. He always includes Mike in what's going on, even though Mike is so limited. The world should take notes from my one-year-old.

Despite how overwhelming and chaotic things can get with two toddlers, they make me see the light. There are so many moments like those I mentioned that I am overcome with joy despite all the heartache. Though, I wonder, how can I possibly feel any sort of happiness when our world is so dark? In all of these moments, I think, Mike should be a part of this. Every morning before we get out of bed, I say, "Today is going to be . . . ," to which Dante responds, "an AWESOME DAY!" The days are hard and exhausting, but at the same time, my heart is so full with the boys. Despite how sad I feel, there are still moments that feel awesome. And sometimes, that makes me feel guilty. I remind myself that if Mike could express how he felt, he'd, of course, want as many awesome moments for us as possible. I am thrilled that despite their obstacles, our boys are such happy, silly little guys.

I know Mike feels the same.

No matter how many thoughts keep me up at night, the one thing I am confident in is that at the end of the day, everyone is very well taken care of and knows they are loved to the moon.

CHAPTER 9

Making Final Memories

I HAD TO ACCEPT THE RECOMMENDATION TO TURN TO HOSPICE, but not all of our family was accepting of that reality at the same time. When hospice first got on board, I literally banned the word itself from my house. He wasn't going to get better, but the ultimate goal at that point was to keep Mike's spirits up as much as possible, no matter what. He was going to die. We all knew it. But as long as he was being taken care of well, why provide him with yet another constant reminder?

As time went on, Mike's acceptance of his mortality grew. As he became more cognitively and physically impaired, he'd plead to higher powers for it to be over. He'd ask the nurse every day, "How much longer do I have?" He wanted relief so badly. And when he started expressing that, we opened up the conversation about death further.

> **Journal Entry from August 16, 2022:**
> *Today, fifteen months after that diagnosis, my husband is on hospice care with a prognosis measured in weeks to a few months.*
>
> *Brain cancer is different from other cancers because full remission is unachievable. The kind of brain cancer that Mike has is one that some people are fortunate to live a long time with, but prognosis often depends on genetic markers and resectability—both of which were not in our favor. Mike fought like*

hell to get through the most brutal of days, but this was never, ever a fair match. Every bit of good news felt like we got in a good punch, but we knew when the match ended, it wouldn't be in our favor. We were forced to stay positive and only celebrate the small wins along the way.

Though it's always well-intended, sometimes telling someone with cancer to keep fighting and not give up is unfitting. Sometimes, to keep fighting means to keep suffering, and being told not to give up leads to feelings of guilt in someone who just wants to be at freaking peace. There is no such thing as giving up. It takes incredible strength to go through cancer treatment, but it takes an equal or greater strength to accept that treatment is no longer what's best when literally all you want is your life back. Collectively, stopping treatment is what was decided with and for Mike.

It's true that I have had a lot of sadness in my life. But I don't have a sad life. My boys will grow up with an inevitable sadness, but they won't have a sad life, either. I've been challenged, but I'm not disadvantaged. I actually feel so blessed, and I still have so much happiness in my life. We go to the pool, we play outside, we visit the zoo, we have dance parties on the couch, and we go out for ice cream (a little too often).

Do I still wish for a miracle for Mike? Do I wish I had my mom's shoulder to cry on over all this? Do I wish they could both be here to help raise the boys? That's a hard yes to all three. Feelings of sadness and grief can absolutely coexist with hope and joy. I'm *somehow living the best and worst days of my life simultaneously.*

Lately, the boys have become total besties and partners in crime. Together, they play, they dance, they chitchat, they cause trouble. I could watch them interact all day, even when they're teaming up to be destructive little monsters. Seeing their relationship develop makes my heart literally explode with the greatest happiness. I've realized that I need to search for and be super aware of moments of joy that come naturally and embrace the opportunities to create more of them.

What's happening to us is sad and unfair, but I really don't want to be a sob story. I know that I've been grieving for the last fifteen months, but I find so much comfort in knowing Mike is still physically here—despite his condition. I can kiss him, hug him, help him. Sometimes, when I give myself the "I can do this" pep talk, I wonder if that strength actually comes from being so numb to my reality. Living in survival mode can do that. I don't know what I'll do when he's gone and it all sets in. Mike told me that I will be okay. That the boys will be okay. That I'm strong and will find a new normal. He told me that I am capable of amazing things and that I will help people on this journey. And so, I have to try.

I have absolutely no idea where this blog will go— but I hope one day it pops up on the right person's screen who may just need to know they are not alone.

Knowing death is around the corner, some would argue, has its benefits. It allowed us to process some of our grief before Mike was gone, but it also allowed us to have conversations about what he was feeling and what he wanted for the kids and me. It gave me an opportunity to "prepare" as best I could. For example, I went out to Target and bought birthday cards for each of our boys' birthdays for every year until they turn eighteen. I sat with Mike in his hospital bed that night with an ink pad. He could no longer use a pen or pencil to write, so with his guidance, I wrote a little note on each card. Then I pushed his finger into the ink pad and signed each card with his fingerprint. I sealed them up and put them away in a safe spot to later gift them on each birthday.

Every day, Mike communicated less and less, though he always gave all his energy to share the I love yous. There was one night in particular when I was sleeping with my oldest in his room and Mike was in his bed in our bedroom with his dad in a recliner not too far away. I woke up to a text that said, "I think tonight is my last night. I love you." It was like Mike had moments of clarity, and I couldn't believe how well-typed out the message was. Usually, it would take some educated guessing to figure out what he was saying or asking for.

Knowing death was close gave us an opportunity to celebrate Christmas all over again. A "re-do," if you will, since Mike was very sick over the last Christmas we spent together.

One day, while playing in the backyard with the boys, my dad said to me, "Why don't we put the Christmas tree up for Christmas in July?"

We thought it would be fun for the kids, so we did. We pulled it out of the basement and brought it up an hour later.

Our angel of a hospice nurse turned forever friend of mine noticed it at her next visit and told a local organization called the Breathing Room Foundation about our Christmas in July celebration. What we thought was a simple, cute nod to the holiday was turned into a full-blown Christmas morning. The organization dropped off a roomful of wrapped Christmas presents after asking what the boys were interested in. There was a water table, a basketball net, a sprinkler, two bikes, and more. The boys wore their Christmas jammies and put out cookies, and Mike's parents and sister were all there with us to watch the boys' faces light up in the morning. It's something we'll remember forever.

There were some beautiful moments that peeked through during those months and weeks. Those moments are what you need to hang onto to survive. To get up. To accomplish your next task. To move forward.

Since we had grown up depending on each other, Mike had a lot of anxiety when I was out of sight in those last weeks. I never wanted to add more stress, so I very rarely left our house. I'd walk the boys to the local pool for a half hour some days, but that was usually it. As I gave myself a little more permission to take short breaks outside of our house, I realized how critical those moments were to our mental health—mine and my kids'. Not only did Mike want me by his side, but my kids also wanted me by theirs. So, me not leaving the house meant they weren't leaving the house. Of course, we'd go out in the backyard to play. And despite the need to be at home, we made a lot of great memories that summer running around and playing with the neighborhood kids.

I managed to take a few quick outings with the boys in those last weeks. We took a brief trip to the Elmwood Park Zoo in

Norristown, Pennsylvania, and went flower picking at Merry-mead Farm in Lansdale. These outings were quick, but they gave us a little break from the sadness at home. Did I still feel a tad bit guilty leaving Mike for an hour? Yes. However, my kids needed a little bit of normalcy. They needed some undivided mommy time. I needed a little bit of undivided time with them, too. These trips not only gave us that, but taking them out by myself and watching them have a blast also gave me a small boost of confidence as a solo parent. *I can do this . . . I can still give these boys a good life . . .*

These small moments, which I sometimes refer to as "grief breaks," are what inspired me to start my nonprofit organization, the Michael L. DiTore Small Moments Foundation, which we'll chat about later on.

CHAPTER 10

Still Tangled Up in You

Journal Entry from September 9, 2022:

Last night, I kissed Mike goodnight, knowing it could very well be the last time I do. Then, I painted the kids' bathroom. I also painted our dining room, and now I'm eyeing up our spare bedroom. Maybe I'm totally losing my mind, or maybe it's boredom. In our old life, Mike and I would go downstairs after the kids fell asleep, pop some popcorn, and binge-watch Catfish—unless, of course, it was Bachelor Monday. Now, everyone is asleep before 7:30 p.m., and I don't know what to do with myself except anything that distracts me from the loneliness of my thoughts. I suppose I am subconsciously—or perhaps consciously—trying to avoid more pain.

A month ago, there was no time to breathe. In between every one of the kids' needs was a need from Mike. It felt like I was responding to physical and emotional needs every minute of the day and, often, the night. Now, Mike's not calling my name because he can no longer talk. I can't make him dinner because he can no longer eat. I needed a break, but now I want that chaos back.

Living in this limbo period is so emotionally confusing. For someone who is so annoyingly Type A, the unknown of this is testing me. It is in my makeup to be "doing." To be planning. I ask the nurse every single day, "How much longer?" but there is no way for them to know the answer. I don't ask because I want Mike to die. I love him with my whole heart and know that a huge part of me will be leaving with him. I ask because he desperately needs and deserves relief. And because it's time for my kids to have some normalcy, as they've already seen and heard more than any toddler should.

The other day, someone asked me how old Dominic was. I said, "He's one," but then followed with, "He'll actually be two next month!"—which is totally absurd in itself. I instinctively thought to myself, How will we celebrate? I felt guilty for having this thought (How can you possibly think about a birthday party right now, you horrible, heartless person?), but one of our nurses, who also happens to be my daily sounding board, reminded me that guilt is for when you do something with bad intentions. Wanting to still celebrate my baby is no reason to feel guilty.

Lately, as we walk through the neighborhood, Dante comments on how excited he is to have so many houses to trick or treat at this year. I love that his innocence allows him to have these kinds of thoughts right now. I don't want anything to take away that innocence prematurely. The boys still deserve to create memories and be celebrated. That's why this is so emotionally confusing!!! I am heartbroken, and I wish the whole world would just take a minute, but with two very young kids, life can't just stop.

In fact, Dante is supposed to start preschool next

week. This next chapter for Dante is so bittersweet for me. It's not so much about the time away from him (because it's literally only a few hours a week), but it's more so that this is the beginning of a new chapter—a chapter of less constant "togetherness." I think I'm struggling because life is changing so much, and it's just another dang thing that I need to let go of.

A physical life with my husband. A two-parent household. Incomplete family vacations and holidays for the rest of our lives. Dante and Dominic growing up despite my constant research on ways to freeze time. These are only some of the things that I'm forced to accept.

Dante has helped me get through the most difficult times in my life. God delivered me this angel baby at a time in my life when I needed happiness. He gave me a new purpose. He needed me, but I needed him, too. Those middle-of-the-night feedings in his rocking chair, just the two of us, brought me as much comfort as they did him. He is three and so dependent on me, but I think I've been dependent on him, too. That makes it hard to let go of this phase of life. The boys' affection is sort of my medicine.

"The human touch is that little snippet of physical affection that brings a bit of comfort, support, and kindness. It doesn't take much from the one who gives it but can make a huge difference in the one who receives it."—Mya Robarts[6]

Dante is kind and caring. He's excited about life. He is so very smart, but more importantly, he is determined and brave, and he thinks hard. He prob-

lem-solves. I can't wait to see all this little boy becomes. Wish us luck. I'm sure I'll be total waterworks in the parking lot as I leave . . . if I leave. ;)

I do wonder why this all has to happen at the very same time, though—the start of preschool, Mike's best friend's wedding, and our sixth wedding anniversary are just a few days away. But I suppose there is no "right" time. Maybe there's just a slightly less horrible time. I don't know.

Lastly, I've always been sort of skeptical of signs from heaven. I've always wanted to believe that some communication could be possible, but I've had a lot of phony experiences in the past. We've always associated my mom with the number five. Her birthday was January 5, 1955, and she used five for everything. Lately, I've looked at the clock at 5:55 p.m. every single day. I was lying in bed with Mike the other day, having flashbacks of when I said goodbye to my mom for the last time. Right after this thought, I grabbed my phone, and BAM—5:55 p.m. I'd like to think it's a nod from my mom, just letting me know she's here and she'll be ready for Mike. Who knows? If it gives me some comfort, I'll let it. It is at least a little weird, though, right?

* * *

Our last wedding anniversary was coming, and it was so very different from our previous five.

For our first wedding anniversary, we took a once-in-a-life-time trip to Italy. We stayed with Mike's family in Rome, where we had homemade spaghetti and meatballs around a table of people who spoke little to no English. We traveled along the

Amalfi Coast and visited the island of Capri. It was the perfect combination of romance and adventure, topped off with good wine and a lot of dark chocolate gelato.

For our second wedding anniversary, we spent a long weekend at Baha Mar in the Bahamas, which also served as our "babymoon" before we welcomed our first son. We swam, ate, and explored the island.

As parents, for our third and fourth wedding anniversaries, we went out to a nice dinner and just spent time together as a family. We'd sit together and rewatch our wedding video and sometimes reread the wedding notes we wrote for each other:

To my beautiful bride,

Our big day is finally here. It's hard to believe, but 440 days later, it's September. The countless days of planning are finally put to rest, and it's time for us to enjoy this special day. It's hard for people to believe that what started out as a high school romance between two fourteen-year-olds grew into the strongest form of love ever imagined. When I look back from the beginning of our relationship until now, it's nothing short of incredible. We went from being afraid of talking on the phone to being a true part of each other's families well before this date . . .

What makes me most excited is that even though we have been together for this long, we are only just starting the rest of our lives together. Whenever I start to envision us with a family of our own, I'm left with the biggest smile. I know that you will not only be the best wife I could ever ask for, but you will be the most incredible mom. I see how great you are with our niec-

es and nephews, and I can't help but think how that
will be our kids one day on the other end of your love.
There has never been something that I've been so
sure about. You are the one person on this earth that
I was meant to spend the rest of my life with. With
my heart beating out of my chest and my stomach in
knots, I will be waiting for you at the end of the aisle.
I cannot wait.
*   With all my love,*
*   Michael*

Every letter was signed "All my love" or "Love always."
The latter is now forever tattooed on my right arm in his
handwriting.

This note is hard to read now. I mean, we were just a normal,
young, happy couple. We had good health and enough money,
and we came from families with strong foundations. All that
bad stuff, like illness and dying young, happened in movies and
to other people, but certainly not to us . . .

For our fifth wedding anniversary, we spent the day and
night in Stone Harbor, New Jersey, at the very hotel where
we had held our wedding reception. Mike was very sick at the
time and still recovering from his first round of radiation, but
we enjoyed a nice dinner, a day together at the spa, and some
much-needed one-on-one time. I actually wanted to do a vow
renewal on our fifth anniversary, but Mike insisted we wait until our tenth. When he said this, I wasn't sure if he believed
we'd see a tenth or if he was just hoping we would.

September 10, 2022, was our six-year wedding anniversary.
I sat on Mike's hospital bed in our living room that day, tasting
the anniversary cake that our hospice nurse had brought over

for us. Mike was no longer able to eat. In fact, I'm not sure what his level of consciousness was or if he could hear anything I was saying. Nonetheless, I lay next to him in that bed, held his hand, stared at that "R" tattooed on his finger, and played some of our favorite songs, including our wedding song, "Tangled Up in You," the lyrics of which are now engraved on his memorial bench at the cemetery.

On September 12, 2022, I took Dante to his first day of preschool. I took all the cute pictures of him holding his back-to-school sign. His favorite color? Yellow. His career ambitions? Become a bigger boy.

Dante walked out that door with a smile on his face, ready to start his new adventure. I cried as I dropped him off because I was so damn proud of his bravery but also because it felt so isolating being one of the only parents who dropped their child off alone. There were moms and dads together, kissing their babies in the hall and taking family pictures at the sign outside the school. I went back home to my husband, whose breaths and heartbeat were slowing every hour, and later left to pick my baby back up and hear about all the wonderful things he did on his very first day of school.

On the following day, September 13, 2022, my sweet husband died peacefully. We all took turns telling him that it was *okay* for him to go. He'd hung on so long already. Our hospice nurse said that while she couldn't explain why, some people want to take their last breath by themselves. Mike was constantly surrounded by family. If I left the room, his mom entered it. But collectively, we decided that maybe it was indeed what he needed to have in order to make his transition. Mike's family went into our backyard to give him a little space while I took the boys up to get washed and ready for bed. As I lay down with them, I realized I hadn't gotten them cups of water like I do every night. I ran back down, took a quick peek at Mike, gave him a kiss, and ran back upstairs to get the boys to bed.

Five minutes.

No more than five minutes passed between the time I ran upstairs with the kids' waters and the time his mom came back inside to check on him again. In those five minutes, Mike took his last breath, and his soul left us. His sister ran upstairs and whispered to me, "He's gone." I didn't want the kids to follow, so I got them to sleep before I came back down. I don't know if it was a coincidence or if it was perhaps some greater force that intentionally determined the timeline of that night. But every single night, my boys would run back downstairs in their jammies to kiss daddy—and whoever else was at our house helping—good night. That night ran differently.

I kissed my sleeping babies, then walked back down to hold my husband's lifeless body. I called our hospice nurse and Mike's cousin, who was also a local funeral director. They came over and pronounced him dead, and it was time for me to let go.

Though it's all a blur at times, I recall falling to my knees in tears, trying hard to catch my next breath. My legs, my lungs, my entire body forgot how to function in those moments. My dad physically carried me out back to get some air while the funeral director brought Mike out to the hearse in our driveway.

I hadn't been able to get through one ninety-minute class in high school without Mike, and now I was expected to live without him for the rest of my life. *Now what?*

CHAPTER 11

Loss Before Loss

I REALIZED IN THOSE DAYS AFTER HIS DEATH HOW MANY MIS-conceptions there are surrounding grief, one of which was that you only grieve after a person dies. I mentioned the term "anticipatory grief" earlier on, but now I'd like to better familiarize you with it. Anticipatory grief is the feeling of grief and loss that occurs before the loss itself actually occurs.

To most people outside of our home, Mike died on September 13, 2022. For some who spoke to him regularly, grief ramped up when Mike was no longer able to communicate by phone. Because I was living it every single day, it felt as though I had lost my husband, the true essence of who he was, many months before the date printed on his death certificate. There are so many losses, both big and small, that you experience with terminal illness before a funeral ever takes place. Our last text message. Our last pregnancy together. Our last phone call. Our last time being intimate. Our last "I love you."

Another misconception is that grief is a linear process. This is far from the truth.

Denial, Anger, Bargaining, Depression, and Acceptance

These are said to be the five stages of grief, and there is no doubt that I progressed through each one of them. I even returned back to some stages based on the trajectory of Mike's illness and how he was feeling.

Denial: When we first heard Mike's diagnosis, I couldn't believe it—my brain just couldn't process the idea of Mike being terminally ill. I was in shock. Our baby was still nursing and had literally just learned how to crawl. Whenever someone would ask how Mike was doing or I was in a position to share his diagnosis, I'd follow a medical update with ". . . He should be okay, though. He'll have to get treatment, and then he'll be able to just live with it for the rest of his life."

He'll just live . . . with . . . brain cancer . . . *no big deal.*

Denial might also look like making future plans. I remember Mike talking about attending Rocky's bachelor party over the summer at a casino in Atlantic City after his second diagnosis. This was denial.

Anger: *Why is this happening to us? Why my kids? Why Mike? This is so unfair,* I thought. *What did we do to deserve this?* I felt angry at our situation and angry at doctors who couldn't tell us what we wanted to hear.

Expressions of anger might look like aggression toward your doctors for not having the answers you want or overreacting to a family member who did something pretty insignificant. It could also look like being rude to the waiter in a busy restaurant who has no control over the speed at which your food comes out.

Bargaining: I spent a lot of time at this stage, reflecting on and second-guessing every single decision we made. I'd think: *The prognosis is a couple of years, but people have lived longer. So, it's not impossible. If we can just keep Mike alive for another ten years, then new medications will be out to cure this thing.*

This could be worse. He could have a glioblastoma (stage four glioma).

What if we had chosen standard of care instead of going right to experimental medicine? Did we go about the whole treatment process wrong?

Maybe he wouldn't have had a recurrence if . . .

Maybe we should have started more complementary therapies sooner.

If the teeny tiny change in his MRI wasn't missed back in February, would he have responded better to treatment?

What if he was treated at this institution instead of that one?

Depression: An immense amount of sadness and defeat consumed me. I didn't know how I could possibly continue walking upon this earth without my husband. My entire life revolved around him and our family. I found myself wishing for other people's problems.

As a result of the depression I felt, I started talking to a therapist, blogging more frequently, and taking antidepressants. I tried to convince myself that I didn't need medication, as if it was a sign of weakness. But the reality was that I couldn't do it all myself. Mike needed me in good spirits to fight for him. My boys needed a happy mommy. I needed a little help, and there isn't a damn thing to be ashamed of about that.

Acceptance: I finally started to process the fact that my husband would, in fact, die. He would not physically be there for the boys and me any longer at some point. What did I need to do to prepare?

I contacted Mike's employer to learn about his life insurance policy. I made a list of passwords for every account we had together, from college savings accounts to Netflix. I made artwork from all of our handprints and fingerprints. I took more intentional videos of Mike and me together and him with the boys. I had conversations with him about my goals, my future, and even about this very book you're reading. Once I accepted the inevitable, I was able to step back from "I'm going to save him" to "I'm going to embrace every moment I can with him."

There is no right way or right order in which to grieve. You don't have to be crying to be sad. As I said previously, I painted my dining room, redecorated my bedroom, and planned my son's birthday party, all while Mike was in hospice care. I was trying to control *anything* I could in a situation that I had no control over. I couldn't control the really sad thing that was about to happen to us, but I could control creating something else to look forward to. I'd exercise and write and pray for Mike to die peacefully. I cope by doing—by staying busy. Others cope by doing nothing. Both are okay.

For over sixteen months, I coped by taking care of Mike. By scheduling his appointments, managing his medication schedule, planning and cooking his next meal, lifting him, washing him, holding him, advocating for him, and calming him. As he got worse, he needed less of me, and as a result, I didn't know what to do with myself anymore.

Making Arrangements

When I realized that Mike only had a few weeks left on earth, I did the next thing that I knew I could do *for* him, which was to identify his cemetery plot. I scheduled an appointment with Whitemarsh Memorial Park, a cemetery located in Ambler, Pennsylvania, which happened to be the same place I had stood next to Mike in my blue, animal-print gown for prom pictures back in high school in 2009. The scenery there is beautiful, and on a nice day, you'll almost always see people running and walking their dogs through there for exercise. I was one of those people. I often wondered if running by while people were visiting their loved ones' graves was wrong, but it became the norm there.

I went to Whitemarsh with my mother-in-law while Mike was at home with his dad and my boys were out to breakfast for their weekly "Pancakes with Pop" tradition.

In one of Mike's lucid moments over his last few months, he told me in great detail what he wanted after he died. I am so grateful that he felt compelled to give me those details because I wasn't sure yet if I'd have the nerve to ask him. He told me he wanted to be cremated, and he told me what to do with his ashes. Let me just say, do yourself a favor and have these conversations *now*. I know it's morbid and depressing, but it's a hell of a lot easier to do when death isn't knowingly looming around the corner. You will do your partner and children an invaluable favor by making this decision for them.

Anyway, when we arrived at Whitemarsh, we went inside to meet with a gentleman who showed me all the options for what to do with an urn. I browsed through his magazine and decided I liked the cremation bench—a memorial bench that has a location to hold an urn. He asked questions like "How many urns do you want to fit in this bench?" and "Do you want your name and birth date on there, too?" It felt eerie to me to have my name on there with an unknown death date, so I passed on that, but I did buy a bench that would fit an urn for me as well. It seemed like the right thing to do at the time.

After choosing a bench, the Whitemarsh employee drove us around in his golf cart to look at various locations around the cemetery grounds to decide where the bench would sit. We stopped in a mausoleum so that I could show them where my mom's urn sat at the time. It's a colorful urn with a funky design that is very fitting for her style. She often wore mismatched prints and bright-colored sneakers, much different than the daily black leggings and gray sweatshirt combo you can find me in at school drop-off. Her urn sat in a glass window next to a picture of her in her thirties, seashells with each grandchild's name on it, and a business card from her children's clothing store called Kid N' Kaboodle, which she opened when I was young with her friend Mary Grace.

I didn't love where my mom's urn sat (as if you could ever really have a love for something like that). I wanted something different for Mike. He was outdoorsy, and somewhere under a beautiful tree where I imagined I'd later sit and have picnics with the boys felt more appropriate for him. We found a spot tucked away in front of some beautiful native rhododendrons (which I could only put a name to because my father-in-law owns a landscaping business). The spot felt as right as it possibly could. I signed the paperwork and texted my sister-in-law, Jess, who is an incredibly talented artist, to tell her my idea for what I wanted to have engraved on the bench, and then I drove back to my husband at home and didn't say a word about where I'd been.

I also wrote some of his eulogy as he was sleeping in his hospital bed right next to me. I wrote half of it in the present tense, "Mike is . . . ," until I later changed it all to past tense after he died.

These things needed to be done, but they also gave me the sense of purpose I was longing for, like I was still doing things *for him* when he didn't really need me anymore. It felt like I was caring for him again.

These were more examples of my search for control over a situation in which I had none.

The truth is, nobody knows what they're doing when they lose a loved one. It's normal to have intrusive thoughts. It's normal to feel a range of emotions. It's normal to find ways to get control back. And it's normal to want to avoid topics of death, though perhaps not always healthy. It's normal to wonder how you're going to log in to the PECO account to keep paying bills each month, and it's normal to wonder what your life insurance payout will be. It's normal to not want to get out of bed, and it's normal to plan and stay busy. Last, it's normal to stop playing superhero and accept death in order to find peace.

The mix of emotions I felt after Mike died felt contradictory. I was utterly heartbroken, but I also felt a huge sense of relief. He was finally free.

The morning after Mike died, the kids walked down the steps for breakfast like they always do. They walked around our house, spending a little extra time in the living room, realizing that the bed, equipment, and daddy were all gone now.

I told them the news.

We'd talked about death. We'd read books about death. But the permanence of death is a nearly impossible concept to understand for a then one- and three-year-old.

I dropped Dante off at school that day and found some comfort in knowing this would be the first day of a new routine. A fresh start. It was the homecoming of *normalcy* in their lives.

I still had calls to make and a funeral to finalize, but our boys didn't have to come home to the tense, depressing situation of waiting for Mike to die.

On the day of Mike's funeral, it felt like the events quickly came and went. I stood in line on September 16, 2022, feeling numb, sharing hugs with people I hadn't seen in a decade and shaking hands with people I'd never met in my life. It was repetitious and exhausting, though I greatly appreciated every single person who came to show support. The line of people wrapped around the church, right next to the preschool my oldest son attended. After the service, we headed to Whitemarsh, where we had a quick ceremony and I placed Mike's urn into the bench I had picked out for us. I asked the funeral director to play "Everybody Talks to God" by Aaron Lewis as we walked toward it.

Across the street from the cemetery, we had a luncheon at Angelo's Italian Kitchen, the same location where Mike had hosted my thirtieth surprise birthday party just eleven months prior. It was a common venue for bridal and baby showers. We know the owner and have a level of comfort there, so . . . Angelo's it was.

The strangest part of the day was that when the luncheon ended, everyone went back to their business as usual when my life and home looked extraordinarily different. I vaguely remember the rest of that day, but I do recall playing in the backyard with my kids afterward and noticed my next-door neighbor, whom I'd seen earlier in the day at the church, over the fence. She complimented me on my speech, and we continued to play on the swing set. I thought about how weird it was that this could all take place on the very same day.

Over the next few days and weeks, my family went back home, and the flowers that had been sent started to wither while new ones stopped coming. People went on with their lives—back to work and back to school. We had to do the same, but there was no "back" to normal. This was an entirely new chapter for the three of us. I started to paint yet another bathroom and find new ways to stay busy each night. I felt a debilitating loneliness but also a sense of freedom. My mother-in-law and father continued to come over, but it all felt different.

Journal Entry from October 25, 2022:

(A letter to my husband)

There is so much I want to tell you. I wonder if you can see Dante's excitement about preschool. His teacher says he's very quiet, but he seems to be slowly warming up. I wish I could be a fly on the wall in that classroom—but I bet you have the best view of all.

Dommy turned two this month, and we had so much fun, but the void was evident. Their innocence is both a blessing and a curse. I know it's impossible for their little brains to process any of it.

I'm told all the time how strong I am. The truth is that my strength comes from having no other choice but to face what's thrown at me, but even more so, it comes from you.

So now, I'm almost two months into this widow thing, and here's what I've learned so far: I've learned how to uninstall and reinstall car seats—which sounds pretty lame, but it was just naturally always a you job.

I've learned that if I go into a situation with confidence, the boys respond better. For example, I weaned Dominic all by myself, which felt like a huge accomplishment, considering I had the luxury of just passing Dante off to you the first time around.

I've learned about headstones and land rights and can use cemetery language like it's part of my day job.

I've learned that I can't plan for everything but can only prepare, and I've learned the importance of a good life insurance policy at any age.

I've learned that you were 10,000 percent yourself everywhere you went. Hearing your coworkers and college friends talk about you solidified what I already knew . . . your authenticity.

I've learned that you don't move on but, instead, move forward.

I've learned how to function in complete exhaustion and that one of my greatest strengths is remaining calm for the kids when I'm actually beyond frustrated.

I've learned that heavy sadness and immense happiness can be felt in the exact same moment.

I've learned to do more of what Rebecca wants to do and care less about others' opinions. You truly can't make a judgment unless you've walked in someone's shoes—and even then, it's never the same.

I've learned that "anticipatory grief" is the term that describes what I've been trying to explain for so long now, which is that my grieving journey began a year and a half ago at the very moment you were diagnosed. When it came to your last moments, I was destroyed but also weirdly relieved . . .

I've learned that while I'm doing pretty well most days, there will always be unexpected triggers. I recently had to go back to the hospital where the boys were born, and it was tough. That hospital is where we walked in as a family of two, then walked out as a family of three, and then again twenty-two months later as a family of four. It's where you held my hand and rubbed my back as I winced in pain. It's where you left my bag of throw-up in the parking lot before we wobbled me into the emergency room (woops). It's where we cried together in fear when Dante's delivery went awry. It's where my dream of a natural VBAC (humble brag) came true despite it feeling impossible, and it's where I thought we'd return one day to walk out as a family of five.

I've learned that there is no right way to grieve. I've been hard on myself for seeming emotionless and frustrated with myself for not snapping out of a sad moment more quickly. It's all okay.

I've learned that it's also okay to think about you and laugh. I bought jeans the other day and smiled because, to you, that would probably be the most concerning thing I've done so far. I've also been going through some of your clothes, and while I'm not quite ready to part with most of them, I've fallen in love with your blue flannel—the one that you've had since eighth grade that I've tried to get rid of eight hundred times over the last six years. I'd tell you how old and ugly it was, and you'd tell me it was going to be a family heirloom. Who would have guessed how much I'd love that thing now?

I left my job because I think there is a benefit to giving the boys all of me right now. I have no idea what's next for me, which is scary and unlike me but also a huge weight off my shoulders. Sometimes, I'm playing in the backyard with the boys and think I will never leave this house, but the very next day, I contemplate if it makes better sense to be elsewhere. I guess that's when I have to remind myself that I can't plan ahead for everything, and for now, I have to sit in the discomfort of the unknown. I don't know. Day by day. I miss you a ton, but we're doing it, and you'd be so damn proud!

P.S. The Phillies are in the World Series (see previous point made on the ability for sadness and happiness to coexist). I hope you are celebrating hard up there, babe!

CHAPTER 12
I Will Survive

When I was a kid, my mom and I spent summers down in Ocean City, New Jersey. Almost every Monday night, we'd walk from our house at 18th and Asbury Avenue to Johnny B Goode Ice Cream Parlor at 1363 Asbury Avenue to sing karaoke in front of fellow ice cream eaters. It was as if we were regulars at the local bar. Everyone knew us. *Every single* Monday night, I'd order mint chocolate chip ice cream and we'd sing the same song: "I Will Survive."

And so, it later became the anthem of my life.

Despite getting knocked down so many times in my life, I never did lose hope. When I could no longer hope for a recovery, I hoped for a peaceful life with my kids, a life in which we'd grieve but also feel joy again.

In May of 2021, when Mike was first diagnosed, I couldn't fathom doing any of it alone. I didn't see a future where I would successfully parent and support two grieving children all by myself. In fact, I used to be afraid to stay home alone overnight—so afraid that if Mike had a night away for work or traveled for any other reason, someone almost always stayed at my house with me in our spare bedroom. Usually, that someone was Mike's sister, Nicole. I'd spend hours thinking about a plan on how I'd save both boys and our dog by myself if there was a fire in the middle of the night. Or I'd think about if someone were to break into our house. *Ok, I'll quickly grab Dominic and bring him into Dante's room. I'll lock the door and move the dresser in front of it while I call 911 . . .*

I couldn't see at the time how I'd do bedtime routines and get two kids ready for school and to doctor's appointments and swim lessons, all as a solo parent.

Solo Parent versus Single Mom

I use the words solo parent because it feels different than being a single mom. The change in my relationship status was fully out of my control—not to trivialize the challenges of divorced parents whatsoever. There are some extreme complexities associated with co-parenting, especially when co-parenting with someone who doesn't contribute equally. But I use the term "solo parent" because I had no "co-parent." No co-financial supporter and no co-decision maker. Sure, I had financial help, and I could call my dad for advice on anything that came up. I could do that because our family loves us and has the ability to support us in those ways, not because they're legally obligated to. Either way, it still came down to me.

I also never felt single. I was alone, and not by choice. When I had to check off the box to identify my relationship status at the doctor's office, "single" and "widowed" were separate options. Plus, when I later joined into a new relationship, I was still a solo parent, but I wasn't single.

Journal Entry from March 8, 2023:
You know how when you're a new mom and your child eats their first bite of sweet potato, you literally think they just hung the moon? Or when you have ninety-nine pictures of your toddler (through the monitor) sleeping with their butt up in the air because you think it's the cutest freakin' thing ever? Every kid does it . . . but not as cute as yours does. The first thing

you do is snap a picture and send it to your partner because they are the only other person on this planet as obsessed as you are with every single move those little humans make. As a new mom, that's what I used to do—all day long.

The other day, Dante wanted me to build a Magna-Tile tower as high as the ceiling while Dominic was loudly and proudly calling me over to show me the five hundred tiny pieces of Play-Doh he cut all over the dining room floor. I tried to divide my attention. I recognize how fortunate I am to have an extra set of hands for at least a couple of hours on most days— which is not the case for every solo parent.

I'm so grateful that I have help when I need it and most of the time when I want it. I'm truly grateful that I don't carry a lot of the other burdens that solo parents often carry (financial struggles, isolation, etc.). Sometimes, it even feels like I should be struggling more to carry such a title. But honestly, I'm just not giving myself enough credit. Because even with a very hands-on and supportive village around, it still comes down to me.

I'm the only one with magical smooches that can fix a boo-boo. I'm the only one popping out of bed at 4 a.m. to someone screaming, "Mommy! BOOGERS!" or at 3 a.m. to clean up chunky, red throw-up all over both the crib and a sad, sleepy little boy.

I am the sole decider of where these boys go to school, what activities to sign them up for, and how much screen time to allow.

I am the tracker of all birthday parties and doctor's

appointments and the one responsible for remembering that Dante needs to bring something that starts with the letter "D" in for Show and Share this week.

I'm the one who bathes them, reads to them, and lays with them as they fall asleep. The one they look for each morning and the one they expect to fill their bellies at breakfast.

I'm the one dishing out enough Pirate's Booty so I can have a moment of silence to add up all the medical expenses for our "jointly" filed tax return—reliving the h*ll that was 2022:

February: hospital bills

March: medical travel to Michigan

May: mileage to and from radiation treatment

June: chairlift installation and rental

September: funeral expenses

I'm the one who must notice that Dante's shoes don't fit anymore or that we're running out of diapers.

I'm the one to clean up the mess Dom leaves behind all day long. :)

I am the one responsible for staying on top of their mental health (as well as my own), and I'm also the primary person in charge of keeping their daddy's memory alive for them.

I'm also the one Dante jumps up and down for when he walks out of school and the only one Dom wants to snuggle with on the couch when he's sick (besides his big bro, if he'd let him).

I'm not writing this to toot my own horn (or maybe I am just a little), but I started thinking the other morning (the 3 a.m. throw-up morning) that I'm do-

ing it—something that, if you asked me a few years ago, I wouldn't have believed I could do. And sure, it's a heavy load to carry. But not being able to share those moments or text that picture to the only person who could possibly care as much as I do, mixed with the unwavering guilt of being present while daddy can't . . . that takes the cake. That ranks high on my list of crappy young widow mom scenarios. This may be a less profound post, but honestly, I'm just here to say don't take that stuff for granted.

The point is, I didn't think I could survive doing any of those things, but *here I am*. I did them, and I'm doing them. I'm surviving.

I started by controlling what I could control. I contacted Dante's school to tell them about our situation. I asked them to please be considerate and use inclusive language when they spoke about families. Thankfully, they were already mindful of this. For example, they had a Father's Day event called "Donuts with Dudes" instead of "Donuts with Dads."

I did the same thing with Dante's coach when he started Quickball last spring. I couldn't control what happened to us, but I could try to control the way Dante and Dominic's environment treated children who had lost a parent by sharing our story.

I also started brainstorming what I could do with my pain and this experience. I wondered what more I could do to help other people. And when I started to open up those thoughts, I was asked by the Breathing Room Foundation (BRF) (the organization that hosted our Christmas in July) to write their 2022 appeal letter. This felt like my first true opportunity to make an impact in the cancer community, so I jumped on it. I wrote a two-page letter telling my story. They sent it out to over fifty thousand families, which raised more money for the BRF in 2022 than letters in any prior year.

I had this overwhelming energy to do something positive with my unwanted experience. I wanted to yell about it from the rooftops. On the outside, I was this sad widow, but on the inside, a fire burned, and I longed to take that sad energy from my trauma and do something positive.

> **Disclaimer:** It's perfectly okay to not feel this way. You don't need to always turn pain into purpose. But this feeling was nagging at me every single day after Mike died. I didn't know what it was, but I had to find constructive ways to let it out.
>
> This appeal letter gave me a little nudge. A little confidence. A little whisper that said, "This is the time. You have an opportunity here. You can do more. Take it."
>
> So, I started with the letter and went from there. The success of it led me to transform my life and my goals, which you'll learn more about later on. I started believing in myself. I had a new sense of confidence. I felt driven and happy and like I could truly take on the world, one word at a time.
>
> **Another disclaimer:** Grief is unpredictable. And as you now know, it's certainly not linear. While I felt this sense of power and motivation, I would still find myself in the car singing loudly to Miley Cyrus one minute and then crying the next because a song from my "sad song playlist" unexpectedly came on.

Sad Song Playlist

My sad song playlist is a list of songs I've compiled that I play when I'm in my feelings or need to really get out a good cry. It includes songs like "Beat You There" by Will Dempsey, "If Heaven Had a Landline" by Brian Congdon, "Life Goes On" by Ed Sheeran, and "You Should Be Here" by Cole Swindell. You can find more of my favorite cry-it-out songs on my website, *www.rebeccaditore.com.*

In spite of still feeling intense sadness, I invited Mike's friends from college over one night to catch up. I hadn't seen them since the funeral. We were drinking wine and having a blast together, and then they announced that they were expecting a baby boy in the spring. One moment of laughter quickly turned to another moment of tears. Of course, I was thrilled for them, but all I could think was, *Mike would be so happy. He's missing everything.*

Around our first Christmas without Mike, someone gifted the boys and me a photoshoot with Santa in a studio decorated like the North Pole. It was so much fun and so very special to have these moments with the boys. They sat and read books with Santa and told him all about what they wanted him to bring that year. We were laughing and doting over their cuteness, and then Santa asked, "Have you been good boys for Mommy and Daddy?"

It felt as though someone punched me in the gut and knocked the wind right out of me. I chimed in quietly with, "Just mommy," and then tried to shift the focus back to their holiday wish list.

These examples show the very unpredictable nature of grief. You can't control what others say and do. You can't control what people might say to young, grieving children. Wrongfully, people naturally assume you're a part of a traditional two-parent household. One second, I'd be laughing, and the next, I could feel sick from grief. Triggers find you when you least expect them to.

We had a similar experience in the grocery store checkout line just after our first Easter without Mike. Dante and Dominic were in the cart, and as they were "helping" place our food on the conveyor belt, an older woman checked us out. She was kind and engaging with the kids, who are ready to befriend every person they pass by. So, they started talking.

"Did the Easter bunny come for you two? Did the Easter bunny come for Mommy and Daddy?" she asked.

My options, when this happens, are to either ignore it and move on or open up the floor for the awkward apologies and pity. Was I supposed to correct her? I had no idea. I changed the topic, and when we got to our car, I told the boys, "Some people don't know daddy died. It's okay if that woman's comment made you feel sad. It made me feel sad, too." Because, I mean, *it is* so damn sad.

You win some, you lose some. That's grief—a constant juxtaposition.

Pieces of a Journal Entry from April 17, 2023:
As I'm navigating grief, life after loss, and solo parenting, I'm becoming even more sure that there is no right or wrong way to do this. There is no guide. However, there are plenty of people who think they could author one.

It's sort of like motherhood. You read What to Expect and all the other parenting books. You go into the hospital and come out with a whole other human you're now responsible for.

"Here you go; don't screw up."

You have absolutely no idea what to do. No one does, but everyone has an opinion. Breastfeed. Formula feed. Nurse to sleep. Cry it out. Stay at home. Work full time. New motherhood is overwhelming, and there's also no guide. However, there are plenty of people who think they could author one.

The woman judging you for nursing in a restaurant probably isn't a mother. And that person judging you for dating "too soon" probably hasn't experienced the pain and loneliness of losing their life partner (bless their hearts). Sometimes, naivety is a gift.

In both motherhood and grief, you're tired, overwhelmed, and oftentimes depressed. You experience so much unwarranted advice and contradicting information.

Don't hold him so much.

Let her cry. It's good for her lungs. (Huh?)

Don't wallow in your grief.

You have to move forward.

He wants you to be happy. But not too happy.

One of my greatest insecurities about how I move forward lies in the fear that if I "appear" too happy, people will minimize the love I had and will always have for Mike. As if to love him and grieve him, I have to be outwardly sadder (mind you, outwardly sadder isn't always an option when you have two kids who need a happy mommy).

It sounds silly just typing that, because that's just not how this works. Everybody grieving does so in their own way, in their own time. Some people don't take their wedding rings off for years. I switched mine to my right hand a few days after my husband died. This isn't because I was signing up for Hinge and ready to go get out there. I just wasn't married anymore, and I felt like I had to rip the Band-Aid off. I also didn't want someone to reference my husband, because then I was left to uncomfortably announce that he's dead or just go along with the conversation, pretending for a hot sec that my life is still "normal." I'm not sure which one hurts more.

Speaking of Hinge, the truth is that I have connected with widows who signed up for dating apps very quickly after their spouses died. And that's okay.

Dating wasn't even on my mind, but I met my boyfriend by happenstance.

There was a really dark period of time after Mike was first diagnosed when I genuinely didn't know how I'd survive. I couldn't eat, and between the fear of what was to come and two wakeful babies, I couldn't sleep, either. While I'll always be in a process of healing, right now, I'm happy. My kids are happy. And that's all that really matters.

Some people are years into this new life they never asked for and can't even think about dating. That's also okay.

It took me six-plus months to take Mike's clothes off their hangers and pack them away. I have no idea if that's perceived as quick or as long. That also doesn't matter.

As I'm navigating grief and life after loss, I'm realizing how very unpredictable it can be. I've been so *excited for Dante to start baseball, but I was a whole mess the morning leading up to his first game. In his uniform, he was literally edible, and I was so freakin' proud of him out on that field, but in the back of my mind, I kept thinking, this is what Mike dreamed of. He should be here. He should be coaching. But instead, I'm emailing Dante's coach to tell him that Dante's dad isn't here and to please be mindful of how he refers to the kids' guardians.*

Anyway, Dante got a hit in his first game, we had ice cream three days in a row, and Dominic had several successful potty trips all in the same weekend . . .

Ebbs and flows . . . but always forward.

* * *

So, like I sang off-key with my mom as a kid down in Ocean City, New Jersey, I will survive. And while I can't promise that you won't have hiccups along the way, you need to know that *you will survive, too.* Gloria Gaynor said it. I said it. And now, I want you to say it. Right now. Out loud.

Say it again.

Because not only will you survive, but you will smile and laugh, and you will surprise yourself by doing all the things you thought you never could.

CHAPTER 13

Universal Intervention

You may forget my silly anecdotes throughout this book, but what I hope you walk away with is validation and a better understanding of grief and its common misconceptions. I want you to know—like, really know—that whatever you need to do to process your grief is okay. Not one single person has walked in your shoes. Even if they've walked in the same style and brand, it's not the same size. Are they HOKAs or Nikes? Personally, I prefer On Clouds, size eight. The point is, your experience is *your experience only*.

At the same time, my goal is for you to feel less isolated in your grief. We've walked in different shoes along the same path. Caregiving and widowhood are lonely roads, but *I see you*. I see the way you're putting everyone else's needs before your own. I see the way you've neglected self-care and have been forced to take a break from doing the "extras" you once enjoyed. I see the way you take a deep breath to release the frustration and the way you do your very best to battle your nervous system and answer calmly when you hear your name for the eighty-fifth time before noon. I see the way you hold back tears and fake a smile for the sake of your partner and kids.

I see you.

I want you to know that things will be okay again. *You* will be okay again. I had no plan at all once Mike died. I just woke up every day and did what I needed to do. I still took my kids to school and their activities. Sometimes I didn't want to. I tried to accept whatever the universe had in store for me, welcoming whatever good might come our way. But I had no expectations outside of focusing on making sure my kids were happy and healthy.

When it feels like the universe has been doing you dirty for a while, it can be hard to give it back your trust. It's like convincing yourself to still marry someone who's already dismantled your loyalty by cheating on you. It felt as though the universe cheated my family and me. But the reality was that, in order to move forward with peace, I needed to give the universe a chance to redeem my story, whatever that meant and however that might look, with signs, people, and opportunities.

Journal Entry from March 27, 2023:

Last year, caregiving was my identity. It was my entire life, from the moment I woke up to the moment I went to bed. While it was the honor of my life to be in that role, it was exhausting. Self-care was non-existent. No matter how many people gave me the airplane analogy (put your mask on first . . .), when you're fighting for someone's life and taking care of three people who are entirely dependent on you, that's simply not possible.

I was in this perpetual funk that seemed impossible to escape. Realizing I wasn't going to magically break free, I knew I needed to make a change. Getting out of that funk meant saying 'yes' more (to visitors, to play dates, to traveling, to going out, to accepting childcare, etc.). And I have.

After Mike died, I left my job of five years and career of ten to take a few months off and reset. To see where life would take me. To trust that something would point me in the right direction. I understand this is not possible for everyone. While it might not be the career that's on the back burner, there will be things that are pushed aside to make time for true healing.

After writing the 2022 appeal letter for the Breathing Room Foundation, I sat down at Starbucks with the organization's director of marketing and was asked if I'd be interested in writing grants for them. I felt lost and was already looking for a career change, specifically one that would allow me to write. I wanted to do something meaningful. Something that allowed me to fuel some of that fire inside of me—the energy I had in *doing* something with all my pain. An opportunity to write and advocate for the cancer community? To help secure funding that would support people going through a cancer diagnosis?

"Absolutely," I told them. It took very little thought. It felt like this was one of the first *universal forces* leading me to where this changed *Rebecca* was meant to be.

Signs

I started opening up my mind to signs. I'm wired to be skeptical of this stuff. I'm over a grand into very disappointing sessions with mediums, never getting the validation or comfort I was seeking. But despite my skepticism, there are some things that have happened to me that feel unexplainable and too coincidental.

I've had a few dreams with Mike in them. One was just before Dante's fourth birthday. In it, I was walking the streets around Jefferson University Hospital, where Mike and I had walked many times, but this time, I was with the boys and my sister-in-law. Along the sidewalk was one of Mike's pill containers filled with all of his medications. I could see the nine red horse pills for inflammation, the four chalky white ones for seizure prevention, and all the others that I had put in there every single day for sixteen months. In this part of my dream, Mike had already been gone for months. But later in the dream, he was back. He and I were walking side by side inside the hospital. He was moving and talking, and it felt so real. I thought that my dream was perhaps Mike letting us know that though it was different, he was there for Dante's birthday in some way.

Another time, I was digging through my closet, trying to clear out things that I no longer used. In my cleaning sesh, I pulled out my wedding album. The boys were so excited, so we lay on my bed, the three of us, and paged through the book. They commented on the pictures of daddy and me kissing and how beautiful my dress was. They pointed out every uncle, cousin, and grandparent in the book.

One page, in particular, is my favorite. The photographer shot a picture of my mom and dad holding each other, gazing at Mike and me dancing our first dance as husband and wife. It's one beautifully tragic love story watching what would soon become another beautifully tragic love story. There is something really special about this picture. Looking at it with my boys made me emotional. It was very likely one of the last pictures that my mom and Mike were both in together—two people in one photo who meant the absolute world to me and whom I'd never see again in anything but a picture. The thought of that really got to me after paging through the album that day. I longed for them.

The very next day, Mike's hospice nurse, Karin, who I mentioned earlier has become a close friend, sent me a text. In her message was an image of a pink treasure chest with pink and purple flowers along with her daughter's name painted on it.

It was the type of chest a little girl might hold jewelry or nail polish in, and she said she thought it was purchased at my mom's old store. Karin found the chest when she, ironically, was cleaning out her own closet. The moment I saw the picture of the chest, I knew my mom painted it. It was like, somehow, the universe made this connection between Mike and my mom that day and sent it my way.

Another time, Debbie, Nicole, Dante, Dominic, and I participated in a walk to honor Mike just a month after he died, and Debbie's random bib assignment happened to be Mike's date of birth.

I also mentioned earlier that we associate my mom with the number five. Well, I checked my word count for this book at 1,555 words, I have fifty-five emails almost daily, and I check the clock at 5:55 more than once a week, even in the morning, which I sure as heck am not doing on purpose.

I think the sign that floored me and challenged my skepticism the most was when I took my boys to do a Mother's Day photo shoot at Lilliput Farm in Schwenksville, Pennsylvania. The boys were looking spiffy in matching blue shirts, and I was in a long white dress with a blue floral print. The place was beautiful. We brought along our "daddy bears," which are stuffed bears made out of Mike's old flannels, and we took a few pictures holding them. After our mini shoot was done, we walked over to see the farm animals. As we approached the fence, most of the horses paid no attention to us—except for one. One horse came over to us immediately. It wanted our attention, and it wasn't leaving our side. It was the only one. After spending a few minutes talking to and petting this horse, it finally walked away to join the others. When it turned around, I saw it had a big "25" marked right on its big brown butt.

Twenty-five . . . Mike's birthday.

Maybe it's all bullshit. Maybe I'm just grasping at straws. Or maybe it's not. Either way, if these otherwise random occurrences make me feel a sense of warmth and comfort for a hot minute, does it really matter?

I'm open to whatever the universe will send for comfort. And I want to believe it. So, I will.

CHAPTER 14
The Truth About Loss

IF YOU'VE BEEN INTIMATE WITH DEATH, YOU MAY KNOW THAT IT quite literally changes you. When someone experiences trauma, not only might their perspective on life change, but their actual brain chemistry changes. Not only did we lose our person, but we lost our own identity. We no longer fit in the world the same way that we did before our loss.

Experiencing the death of someone close to us can make us want to slow down and enjoy small moments because we know first-hand how fleeting they can be. However, experiencing death so closely can also make us want to live urgently because we know first-hand that we're all on borrowed time.

When Mike was sick, any weekly or monthly plans we made got interrupted. One night, Debbie came over to watch the boys while Mike and I went out to dinner. It had been a long while since the two of us went out. We got our shoes on, and as we collected the things we needed to step out the door, Mike had an unexpected urge to throw up. He ran to the bathroom, and the bathroom is where he stayed. We took a raincheck for our date night but never had a chance to cash it in.

Mike bought tickets with his friends to see Limp Bizkit (his very favorite band) in May of 2022, but his tumor had other plans.

My point is, there was no planning anything outside of medical care. We were forced to live day by day and find moments to enjoy right there at home. We had no idea what the following day or week would bring.

At the same time, death can make you want to wholeheartedly pursue the things that come into your path that bring you joy. You've lived (or may currently be living) through hell. You deserve every bit of that joy.

Death can make you want to honor your loved one in every way possible while also moving forward and rebuilding your own life. I often consult with my dad when I make big life decisions (or even small ones). I texted him for some kind of confirmation before I sold my house, and he responded, "Build your life and don't look back." And damn, have I taken that to heart. I take those words with me everywhere I go. I also take every opportunity I can to share Mike with the world.

We began the annual Mikey D Memorial Golf Outing in 2023. Our inaugural event was hugely successful, and it was beautiful to have so many people from every phase of our life together in one room, all because they had one thing in common: a love for my late husband. This event is meant to honor Mike; talk about Mike; and, most of all, serve as a special tradition for Dante and Dominic to hold onto as they grow. I mean, I want the whole damn world to know who my husband was. I want him to be talked about, honored, and remembered for the incredible human being that he was. But I can't *just* do that. I also need to keep moving forward. I need to rebuild a life that was shattered to pieces. While I cannot live in the past, I can carry the memories of the past with me on my journey forward.

I can, and I must.

We must.

Common Misconceptions

Speaking of moving forward, do you know what gets me really fired up? Opinions from others on *how* we move forward. Some people may believe that moving forward means you don't care about your past. Others may believe that lingering in your grief for more than a year means you're stuck. One major misconception about grief is that there's some rigid timeline someone should follow. It's said that the deepest grief exists in the first six months after loss. But that was just not true for me. In fact, my deepest grief was probably in the first six months after my husband was diagnosed but still alive. *Cue: anticipatory grief.* The timeline of grieving is so vastly different for someone grieving a person who falls terminally ill versus someone grieving a person who dies unexpectedly in a car accident on the way home from work.

Six months? To me, that is so arbitrary.

I've also read online that most people "recover" after one year. Recover? You don't "recover" from grief. If you had love for that person and the loss is permanent, then so is the grief. You learn to live with it. I've had other widows tell me that they felt some pressure to be "back to normal" after one whole year went by. But the thing is, there is no normal anymore. We work to create a new routine, but every single thing about life after the death of a spouse is abnormal and nontraditional.

In fact, I'd argue that it was after one year passed that the deepest parts of my grief resurfaced. The first year is filled with a lot of padding from the support, flowers, cards, and messages, but around one year, the shock of the loss and the attention surrounding it dissipates for people on the outside. For those on the inside, the wound is still so fresh. And far less protected by outside noise.

There is also a misconceived timeline expectation when it comes to the surviving spouse dating again. After spending some of my childhood and then my entire adult life with my late husband, I couldn't begin to conceptualize the idea of dating again. I shouldn't say "again," because the truth is, I'd never really dated before at all. After Mike died, forming a relationship with someone was not on my radar. But the life of a caregiver can be really freaking lonely, so if it is on your radar, I don't blame you. You crave companionship and affection—you're only human. Though, I'd be lying if I said I didn't sometimes wonder what dating again would be like one day. Hell, I was thirty years old.

Within the first few months after Mike died, I was venting to Brooklynne (the same dancing queen from my college breakup) over text message on a particularly difficult night after I put the kids to bed. The loneliness was all-consuming. I needed a friend.

She told me about her cousin, Matthew, another thirty-some-year-old parent of two whose life was collapsing right in front of him, but for a different reason. I felt some weird comfort in knowing I wasn't the only one going through something traumatic at this age. Like, both our lives are an absolute shit show—solidarity, dude!

Feeling lonely isn't a reason to bring a partner into your life—in fact, I think you need to be comfortable being alone first. I went through a lot of discomfort to find the independence and confidence to not depend on a partner or co-parent. However, feeling lonely *was* a reason for Matthew and me to connect and create a friendship. So, thanks to Brooke, we did. No strings attached. No pressure.

We talked about our kids, the unpredictability of life, and what had brought us to this point in our lives. We found irony in the fact that we had gotten married just a few weeks apart and could have been next door to each other when our second children were born in the very same hospital just two days apart.

We talked for hours. And then for days. Over time, it became a little fun and flirtatious. I had no expectations, but it made me feel alive again in a way I hadn't felt in a really long time.

The thing about talking to someone after experiencing something like divorce or death is that there is no time, interest, or energy for small talk. Relationships move much quicker when both partners have experienced grief in some way. You get into conversations in three weeks that may take other, less complicated relationships three months. It was quick and unexpected, but things moved along. However, the anxiety of the possible disapproval from others was a huge distraction from my joy. I feared that someone would dare try to trivialize the deep love I had and will always have for Mike if they knew I was spending time with another man so soon.

A few years prior, after my mom died, I couldn't wrap my head around my dad dating again. It felt selfish. I felt it was "too soon." To me, it felt like a betrayal. I had so many feelings toward it, but I know now better than ever that you really don't *know* until you *know*. And gosh, while we widows want to be understood, we really don't want you to truly understand. Ignorance, in this case, is a gift, because the only way to truly understand widowhood is to live it—and I wouldn't wish that on my worst enemy.

There is no timeline in grief, and I don't know that you're ever "ready" to date again after loss, because grief is not something you ever overcome. However, I think if someone is willing to support you and make space for your healing heart, and they bring you the laughs and happiness you deserve, then there's no harm in it. Who is *anyone* to dispute that?

You have enough love to give. So, if you feel inclined to get out there in the dating world, then here's your encouragement to do it.

Journal Entry from May 21, 2023:

Dear Michael,

It's been two years since we laid in that hospital bed together.

I found a recording of our very first appointment at Jefferson on May 19, 2021, the appointment that led directly to hospital admission for your brain biopsy two days later.

The doctor says, "So, tell me what's been going on," and you begin the elevator speech about how your symptoms have progressed. A speech we gave at least three hundred times over the next several months.

We had no idea what was about to transpire when we walked into the office that day. How beautifully heart-wrenching it is to hear your voice in that audio— filled with naivety.

It's been exactly two years since the doctor called me to tell me your surgery went well but that those lesions on the MRI were, in fact, brain tumors.

It's been two years since I was faced with the reality that I'd be raising these boys without you—that you would likely not be here to see the boys graduate from college, high school, or even preschool. The only thing more difficult than coming to that realization was watching you come to that very same realization.

It's been two years since I began grieving the beautiful life we had planned—the babies, the trips, the vow renewal.

Gosh, you'd be so proud of these boys.

Dante is more confident. He's outgoing. He tells his class and his teacher about his weekends. He's a little jokester at swim class, and he's become so much more comfortable on the baseball field. He says hi to everyone everywhere we go. He is excited to leave me and sleep over at Pop's or Mimi's once in a while.

Dominic just isn't a baby anymore. He talks in full sentences, and he rides his bike without help. He's our little social butterfly with a bold personality that can't be ignored. He wants to do everything his big brother does, but he wouldn't dare get lost in his shadow. He's brave and strong-willed and makes us laugh constantly.

I think about this week two years ago, and I think about everything you're missing out on.

I still wake up some mornings with my heart pounding out of my chest because everyone around me is dying in my dreams. I texted your best friend first thing in the morning to make sure he was okay, because my dream was so vivid, and I couldn't catch my breath. You were there, too.

I've been cleaning out our house and going through notes and cards that we wrote each other. "Here's to another fifteen . . ."

It's been almost nine months without you, but it feels like nine years. Then again, the feeling of my body collapsing as I was forced to leave your side plays in my head like it was yesterday.

So much in my life has changed since that night. So much of me has changed since that night. I've faced so many fears, and I've done so much more than I ever thought I could.

This weekend, I cried because I miss you and can't

comprehend how it's been two years since we got that news. Within the same twelve hours, I laughed my butt off at a comedy show with people that I've quickly come to love.

I'm happy for our happiness, but I also feel guilty. I have excitement for the first time in two years, and that also makes me feel guilty.

That's the weird reality of grief.

I often wonder what you'd think about our life right now. I know that you know that relationships are hard to process after a loss—you know best how hard it was for me after my mom died. But I've come to believe that if you and my mom can see what I see . . . then I know you are both relieved. I know you are both proud of us.

I've realized that it's not about what should be or who it should be . . . Moving forward is about finding the very best out of what is. That's all we can control. Plus, how could more love ever be a bad thing?

Anyway, we're doing it. And I think we're doing it pretty well.

But I miss you.

Love always,

Reebs

* * *

I saw this quote once: "In the happiest of our childhood memories, our parents were happy, too." —Robert Breault.[7]

Forcing out opinions that stem from these common misconceptions can be a tall order. But as I've been reminded many times, *this is my life to live*. And if I make the *wrong* decisions?

They're *my* mistakes to make. I've earned that right. I have two little boys that deserve a happy mommy, and I'd be damned if I let someone else's opinion interfere with that.

Dear reader, when you find yourself at that crossroads, and the opinions of others are creeping in to steal your well-deserved joy, ask yourself if the people with the opinions are actually impacted by the decision you're making.

The answer is usually no.

You deserve to follow your own joy after the amount of sadness you've experienced. And it's damn possible to feel joy and sadness in one day. Hell, in one moment, even. To quote Leo from the movie *Grease*, arguably one of the greatest movies of all time, "The rules are *there ain't no rules*."[8] But there are certainly lessons that you are forced to learn. So, as you move forward, allow the universe to intervene and put the opinions of others aside.

Do what feels right and go live your life, my friend.

CHAPTER 15

Lessons from Grief

As I continue to live my life, I'm somehow grateful for the lessons I wish I never learned.

Lesson One

Grief taught me to let go of the things I cannot control. The only things that come from trying to control a situation over which you have no control are frustration and anxiety. Bad things will happen, and you can freeze up and let them take over your mind and body, *or* you can take the next step to deal with them.

I grew up with a pretty severe case of hypochondria. I self-diagnosed every ache and pain I had as something life-threatening. I had a twitch in my eye for a few weeks in high school, and I convinced myself I had a brain tumor. It was the *only* thing I could focus on, and by obsessing over it, I actually created more symptoms in my head that aligned with the list of brain tumor symptoms I read online. I'd read that *numbness* is a common symptom, and then I'd actually convince myself that I felt numbness in my hands and legs.

I don't know exactly why I was like this, but I do know that grief has changed me. As I mentioned, when Mike was first diagnosed, I had a debilitating fear of something happening to *me*. I thought, *If Mike's down for the count, my presence is even more critical.* I'd make up different narratives about the destruction my uncontrollable absence would cause my kids and their futures.

Even though the pressure to be healthy and safe is heavier now with kids, grief has freed me of that anxiety. I've been more aware than ever of my shortcomings because I don't want to pass the unnecessary anxiety that I grew up with onto my kids. They have their own fears and worries that don't need to be exacerbated by mine. If I'm wrapped up in what else *could* go wrong, then I'm not being the present mommy that I strive to be every day.

Childhood grief can manifest in so many different ways, one being a fear of the surviving parent dying, too. That's valid. Who can blame them? What do you say when your toddler wonders if you're going to die, too? Like, "Yes, sweetheart, yes . . . One day. We're all going to die one day. But mommy isn't going to die right now." At least, I don't think so. Unless a meteor hits our house right now, or I have some undiagnosed heart condition that drops me dead without warning. Could I get hit by a car tomorrow? I could. But, of course, I don't plan on dying anytime soon. I plan on living a really long life. But I can't promise that, of course, because I know damn well that tomorrow isn't guaranteed, and I don't want to go out of this world with my kid feeling betrayed by my promise of a mommy who is immortal. *It's complicated.*

After speaking with the professionals, I've been educated to answer such a question by saying, "Daddy was sick, and his body stopped working. Mommy feels healthy and hopes to live until she is a very, very old lady!" It's like a little assurance but no impossible guarantee. My fear of leaving them too soon is real, but while I will stay on top of my health, wear a seatbelt, and get preventive screenings and annual blood work, I can't control what I can't control.

Worrying about what may or may not happen to me on my drive to pick my kids up from school tomorrow will only ruin the moment that is guaranteed to me right now. When I have irrational fears, I often think back to what a therapist once told me. She said, "When you have this anticipatory anxiety about something, pause and ask yourself what evidence you have to support your worry, and what can you do to prevent it from happening?" If the answer is, "I have no evidence, and there is nothing that I can do to prevent it," then it's not something worth my time, as it's not something I can control. The things that I *can* control and that are, in fact, the reality of "now" are what deserve my energy. I owe that much to myself and my children.

I tried to control Mike's cancer. I thought if I found the right doctor and the right trial and the right combination of complementary treatments, then I could drive the bus. I could outsmart that stupid, ugly brain tumor. But as soon as I let go of control and trusted that I did everything I could to extend his life, I was able to enjoy my husband as my husband again, knowing that his fate was not in my hands.

As for my kids, I can't control my destiny, but what I can do is be present for them in the moments that I'm here and prepare with a last will and testament, a solid life insurance policy, and some financial security for them.

Lesson Two

Grief has taught me to slow down enough to feel grateful for the small, mundane things.

After Mike died, I was going through his phone and came across a note. It was a note I also shared in his eulogy on September 16, 2022.

The note was titled "Things to Never Take for Granted," and it listed the following:

- walking unassisted
- taking a bite of food and swallowing
- walking into the bathroom and walking out
- hearing out of both ears
- walking upstairs
- picking up my boys
- getting in and out of the car

If you stop and think for a minute, you've probably done most, if not all, of these things today without even realizing it. I know I still often do because, truthfully, it's hard to appreciate some of these everyday activities until it's too late.

Do me a favor. If you have the ability to walk, slow down. Feel the ease of one foot moving in front of the other. If you have the ability to drive, think about how it feels to hold your steering wheel. Think about how it feels to have the freedom to get in the car and drive yourself to work or the gym. Think about how it feels to drive your child to school in the morning and to run to a fast-food joint to grab a bite to eat when you're hungry.

Next time you have a glass of wine or a cold beer, sip it slowly. Next time you're out at a restaurant ordering your favorite meal, savor each bite. Next time you hear your little (or big) baby cry with your own ears, take a breath and embrace it. It's frustrating, I know. But imagine if you couldn't hear them cry ever again. Or laugh, for that matter. And even though they might be getting heavy, hold on to them a little longer. Carry them around, even if you're just in the house. Dance with them in your arms in the middle of your kitchen.

Those activities are, in fact, huge privileges.

In Mike's last few months, he couldn't even walk to the bathroom himself. Each step felt like a mile sprint directly uphill. His arms, which he had worked so hard to build up through weight lifting, became too weak to hold his own babies. A man who loved nothing more than eating a good, meaty, flavorful meal was forced to sustain himself on bottles of Ensure. His freedom was ripped away, and he had to rely on someone else for every single desire or need.

Slow down today. Recognize just how *able* you are and find gratitude for those abilities.

Lesson Three

Grief taught me to be kind and give others a little more grace.

Some of my favorite lyrics of all time, not only because I am a crazy Disney-obsessed mom but also because they are incredibly powerful, are from the Pocahontas song "Colors of the Wind." The song talks about how eye-opening it would be to have the chance to walk in a stranger's footsteps. By doing so, you'd learn things you didn't even know you didn't know.

Mike would often go to Alliance Cancer Specialists in Horsham, Pennsylvania, to get an IV of fluids, which took approximately two and a half hours to complete. He'd sit there bored out of his mind, scrolling social media. There were many times that I sat right there with him for the whole infusion. Sometimes, I'd run out to grab him a Frosty from Wendy's or whatever else he was craving that day.

One day, I stepped out to grab him a soft pretzel, which, besides homemade French toast, was something he craved often. It was also something he could more easily stomach with his persistent belly issues. I left him with the IV that day, knowing the sweet nurses there would take care of him. I drove down the street in my black Jeep Cherokee to the Philly Pretzel Factory, just a few minutes away on Horsham Road. As I waited in line to give my order, I saw a sign on the counter that said: "Today, you may be standing next to someone who is trying their best not to fall apart. So, whatever you do today, please do it with kindness."—Unknown

Tears filled my eyes. *Me! That's me! I'm the person you're standing next to, doing my best to do just that.* I felt so seen and so alone at the very same time. Part of me felt like, yes, this quote was made for people like me. I seem tough as nails, but damn, am I fragile. *Are you people really believing this big cheesy smile on my face?*

At the very same time, it felt lonely standing in a place where no one knew anything about me. The gentleman behind me could have never guessed what was happening back at home. Maybe for him, it was another uneventful day in the office, and he was grabbing snacks for his coworkers. Or maybe he was bringing a pretzel home to satisfy his pregnant wife's craving. I'll never know. But I do know that whether we're facing an angry driver who just cut us off or someone who seems rather impatient waiting in line at the grocery store, we should pause before we react. Not only do we have no idea where they're rushing to or what's waiting for them at home (unless they tell you, of course), but getting worked up isn't worth our energy either.

Be a kind human.

Lesson Four

Lessons four and five are directed toward the village around you. Share these lessons; the chapter; or heck, even the whole book with the people who will inevitably ask you, "How can I help?"

I say this because grief taught me how to best support people suffering from illness and loss. We caretakers and grievers have very little time to focus on cooking. The only time I consumed a home-cooked meal that wasn't heated dino nuggets with macaroni and cheese was when a friend, family member, or neighbor dropped one off. With my two cute little picky eaters and Mike's dietary restrictions, I was left eating whatever was left over from their meals. Or I didn't eat at all. Receiving meals at our door was so helpful.

Sending groceries also reduces some burden on the family. Back in chapter 8, I shared a blog post I wrote about my life as a caregiver in the summer before Mike died. As I mused about the mental load of caregiving, I wrote, "It's remembering what food staples we're out of because if we go *one day* without applesauce or waffles, the boys might chop my arm off." After I posted this, someone went shopping and dropped off waffles and applesauce at my door.

That, my friends, is a perfect example of what you can do to show support. If you don't have the specifics of their grocery list, ask. Send a text that says, "I am going to the food store. Tell me what you need, and I'll drop it off at your door after."

For kids, drop off age-appropriate toys. A sweet family from my past held a lemonade stand to raise money for a monthly subscription box filled with educational and engaging activities for the boys. It was a sweet surprise for us every time we saw it at our front door. Plus, what a wonderful lesson those parents gave their three young children that day as they sold lemonade to their neighbors with us in mind.

A few friends chipped in on a home cleaning service for me, which was immeasurably beneficial for my mental state. A clean house felt orderly—unlike most of my life. I was living in survival mode, and cleaning my house was last on my list of priorities. I highly recommend this as a way to help a family dealing with illness or loss.

My favorite gesture of all? Food and grocery delivery gift cards! The downside of having food dropped off was that we often received more than we could handle, leaving some to go to waste. If you don't know what someone likes to eat, gift cards are the way to go. Having the ability to quickly order myself a salad to eat at my convenience was incredibly helpful.

However, before you drop off groceries or a gift, text them and tell them, "I'm dropping something off at 3 p.m. today," and then at 3:02 p.m., text them, "It's at the front door!"

Offer these specific ways of helping.

If you can't manage to send any of these things, send kind words. The reality is that there are no perfect words that will fix their circumstances. Here are a few things you *can* say:

"I'm thinking of you constantly."

"This is unfair."

"This really sucks. I'm so sorry that this is happening to you."

"I will never pretend to know what you're going through, but I'm supporting you every step of the way."

The loss of a middle-aged parent or grandparent is heartbreaking. I've experienced both. But I assure you, the loss of a young spouse and partner is very different. Though it was meant well, it was actually hurtful and irritating when someone would try to relate those experiences.

In addition, share a memory of their person that is special to you. I received countless messages from people (some of whom I've never met) who shared the ways Mike impacted them. These messages were invaluable to me, and I hope they will be to my boys one day, too, when they ask about the kind of man their dad was.

Just as important as what to do, though, is what *not* to do.

Lesson Five

Grief also taught me what *not* to do to support people suffering from illness or loss. First and foremost, doing and saying *nothing* is the worst thing you can do. Don't make it about *you*. Saying nothing because you "didn't know what to say" is, honestly, a selfish cop-out. It's not about you and your comfort. If you feel speechless, say, "I am at a loss for words, but I am thinking about you."

That's okay to admit, and it's lightyears better than silence. I promise that silence doesn't go unnoticed. I may have hardly had time to catch my breath, but somehow, I was still very much aware of who stepped up for us and who dropped the ball. And that sticks. I certainly didn't know the right words when we found out Mike was sick or when they told us it was incurable. I didn't know what to say to Mike, my family, or my kids. I felt a level of discomfort that I'd never felt before—a discomfort that physically consumed every inch of my body. But those who have experienced illness and loss have sat in situations far more uncomfortable than the one you're in, considering what text message to send.

Additionally, avoid *toxic positivity*. According to the Anxiety and Depression Association of America, "Toxic positivity occurs when encouraging statements are expected to minimize or eliminate painful emotions, creating pressure to be unrealistically optimistic without considering the circumstances of the situation."[9] For example, in an extremely sad and painful situation, comments like "Everything happens for a reason" or "He's in a better place now" are inappropriate. They make the person on the receiving end feel invalidated.

When you lose someone so close to you that every minute of every day is forever altered by it, you don't believe there is a reason for it. It feels like really shitty, horrible luck. It's as though someone closed their eyes and ran their finger up and down a list of names until someone yelled "Stop!" They opened their eyes, and their finger was on Mike. No rhyme or reason for it. And with two young children, there really wasn't anywhere better for Mike to be than right here with our new family. That's what I wanted. That's what Mike wanted. That's what our boys wanted. I mean, shoot, he was thirty years old with an *entire life ahead of him.*

Don't try to find some silver lining in our bad luck. Just validate the suckiness and stay there with us. Acknowledge that you can't even fathom the amount of pain we're experiencing.

Send a gift or a text, but don't ask us what you can do. "Let me know what I can do for you" is assigning an unnecessary chore to someone who can hardly manage to successfully finish a load of laundry on the first attempt. It comes with good intentions but doesn't land that way. More times than not, you'll get a generic answer: "Thanks, I will." But we won't. Because we've already put our phones down to run to the next task that you simply cannot do for us.

Per lesson four, do drop off a meal or gift, but do not ring the doorbell or ask them to meet you at the door. I couldn't go to the bathroom alone, so having to escape my children for five minutes for small talk was not making it onto the agenda. It makes an otherwise very nice and generous gesture burdensome.

Last, expect nothing in return. Don't expect a thank you— or a response at all, for that matter. Let people grieve and not feel responsible for the "extra" stuff. This is not a baby shower. If you're truly trying to help, then be okay with that. If you're bothered by not receiving a timely thank you, then reconsider why you're making the gesture—to ease the burden of the suffering family or to make yourself feel better. I promise we're so very thankful.

If you've done these things before, fine. It's okay. You meant well, but now you know how to have more of an impact.

Some of this may come off as harsh, but cancer and caregiving for someone who has cancer is harsher.

Pieces of a Journal Entry from August 29, 2023:

I can feel September creeping in. One whole year without you. Without touching you. Without smelling you. Without staring at the "R" permanently inked on your ring finger.

Our seventh wedding anniversary is right around the corner.

In the last 350-plus days, it feels like three lifetimes have passed by.

I've learned that when you are the one in the receiving line at a funeral, and the one picking out the urn, and the one watching someone (your someone) who "did everything right" in life be completely robbed of their future . . . you see life much differently.

The unpredictability of life used to scare me. So much so that it became debilitating at times. But grief has taught me to let go of the things I can't control. And that's been insanely freeing. So, instead of obsessing over that unpredictability and over all the other things that could go wrong, I try to focus my thoughts elsewhere . . .

I think about the way Dante and Dominic greet every person we pass by. And I think about the elderly woman at the library who said my children made her day just by introducing themselves.

I think about the determination Dante had in casting a fishing rod for the first time and the way they both fearlessly run into the ocean, ready to battle waves.

I think about the excitement I saw on their faces when they caught a lightning bug for the first time this summer and the way they sing at the top of their lungs without a care in the world.

I think about the way Dominic asks me to fluff his pillow in a very particular way each night and the way he holds my hair to help him calm down when he's upset.

I think about the pride Dante has as he notices the improvement he's made in writing his letters . . .

Grief taught me to nurse these moments. To let it be these thoughts that consume me instead of the "what ifs."

Looking back, 2021 and 2022 nearly broke me. I was living in pure survival mode every second of every day. I cried and cried, and I pleaded with higher powers to change our situation. I would have done anything.

2023, though . . . 2023 has been a year of hope, healing, and rebuilding. In the last year, I threw birthday parties, I cooked a turkey, and I still created a magical Christmas morning. I took Dante to school on time every day, I weaned Dominic in the fall, and I potty-trained him over the summer. I survived another 350-plus nights of interrupted sleep.

I've taken the boys to therapy and on vacations, and I watched them fall in love with the Jersey Shore, *just as I dreamed about growing up.*

I rejoined the gym, and I've taken time for myself.

I've cried to my husband at the cemetery, and I've smiled at him in my dreams.

I've become more confident and outspoken, and I've found purpose outside of motherhood.

I've built new, meaningful relationships with people and have been forced to let others fade away.

I've grown, and I've faced fears, and I've bravely opened up my heart to love again.

I've let go of what others think, and I've learned the true capacity to feel pain and joy together in one moment.

I'm giddy and happy and sad and excited. I feel incomplete but also at peace.

I'm relearning what partnership and companionship feel like.

I learned how much I'm truly capable of, and though I want to do all the things, I know I don't have to do all the things.

I've had to snap out of the mentality that I'm less of a mom if I don't do it all myself, because no one person can do all the things. In the last year, I've cheered through a season of little league, rallied on the sidelines of the soccer fields, and sat proudly through weekly swim lessons. We've been to the zoo and the boardwalk, and we've crossed off almost every item on our summer "to-do" list (we have two weeks left!).

When winter turned to spring, I had flashbacks of the trauma the previous two springs brought on. I used to feel such excitement as the weather warmed up, but this year was different. The excitement over more time outdoors with the kids was overshadowed by the memories of our hospital stays and the walls of the radiation oncology waiting room. It was overshadowed by the sound in my head of Mike choking on every bite he took and the images of the medical equipment all over my house.

I can feel the pain and fragility of September approaching as the weather changes from summer to fall and as I prepare the boys for their first day of school.

I'm not yet sure how I'll spend those "firsts" yet . . . but I do feel as though if I can just get to the other side of September . . . there is a much-needed fresh start waiting for us.

So much can change in one year . . .

Finally, don't disappear after a year. Don't ever *stop* checking in. Grief doesn't go away, but without continued support, it does begin to feel unseen. And there is healing in feeling *seen*.

If people understood grief just a little bit more, I think they'd have more kindness in their hearts, dish out less grief-related judgment, and just maybe have a new sense of ambition to go after the things they want in this life.

Lesson Six

Grief has taught me to believe in myself and dive in.

I didn't really know my purpose in life outside of motherhood. Raising my babies was the only purpose I felt I needed when they were born. I struggled to find passion in my career because I was so anxious and hyper-focused on my excitement to start a family.

I watched Mike talk and dream about fatherhood. I watched that dream come to life when he held our babies for the very first time. I watched him hold Dante's hands as he took his first steps in the street out back of our townhome in Lansdale.

I heard him talk about all the future experiences he couldn't wait to have with Dante and Dominic—like taking them to their very first Phillies game or to the hunting cabin in Potter County that I spoke about earlier. It was a small cabin with several sets of bunk beds inside, where thirteen or so men would spend their nights playing poker, drinking, and talking. Each Thanksgiving weekend, they'd fall asleep in these tight quarters until it was time to pull out their rifles in the morning. Mike first went up to this cabin with his dad at the age of eleven. He couldn't even hunt until the following year, but the trip was as much about bringing a buck back as it was about spending time with his dad, uncle, and cousins—a true "guy's" weekend.

Over the course of Mike's illness, I painfully watched him come to the realization that not only would he never take the boys to their first game or see them shoot their first buck, but he likely wouldn't even see them blow out the candles on their very next birthday. I quietly prayed, "If he can live just ten years, he'll get at least one trip in with them and live out that dream . . ." Bargaining once again.

Witnessing this made me realize just how precious and short this life can be, motivating me further to just dive in and swim directly toward what I want out of this life.

In addition to these dreams, Mike had big career aspirations, though after getting sick, they went from climbing the ladder to rehabbing his fingers enough so he could use his keyboard to do the bare minimum. The bare minimum was *never* Mike's style.

I watched him work his ass off every day in the gym. He'd write down his weight and track his progress. He had goals for his health and his body, but the tumor growing in his brain fought against him once again.

My point is, I watched Mike's dreams be ripped away from him at the age of twenty-nine. I don't know how long I have here on earth, but I'm sure as hell going to use my time wisely. I'm going to work toward *my* goals to honor the goals Mike never had a chance to work toward.

So, here we are today, and you're holding in your hands this book that I dreamed about. A book I thought about for a long time but wasn't sure I could actually pull off. Before deciding to make this book a reality, I thought heavily about what others would think. Who am I to think I have something worth reading? Impostor! It all felt out of reach until I just said "yes" to myself. Until I decided to *believe* and *dive in*.

As I briefly mentioned earlier, I also founded a new nonprofit organization called the Michael L. DiTore Small Moments Foundation. Our mission is to create small moments of joy for children who've lost a parent or sibling to cancer. You can find our website and social media at the end of this book.

For the first time outside of motherhood and caring for Mike, I had found something I was truly passion about. I was driven toward this mission. I started the organization because after Mike died, getting out of the house to adventure with my kids—whether it be to Legoland, the Crayola Experience, the zoo, or the nearby farm—served as some of our very first steps toward healing. Finding *small moments* of joy with my kids through these experiences gave me a sense of renewal, and they enlightened us with the life-changing truth that we *can* still laugh and have fun, even when we're really, really sad. These experiences gave my kids a sense of normalcy and helped us to create beautiful memories together in our new dynamic, even during a very dismal time.

My intimate relationship with death has taught me to first believe I can and then act upon that belief with urgency, whether it be with the book, the job, or the relationship. We have one shot at this. No re-dos.

Why worry about the opinions of others? Why not dive the heck in?

CHAPTER 16

Your Next Steps

I RECOGNIZE THAT LIFE'S BEEN EXTRA HARD FOR YOU. I KNOW peace, joy, and any form of relaxation might feel so far out of reach. Healing sounds impossible. I know the thought of having *one more thing* added to your plate is overwhelming. But stay with me.

There are four critical steps that I took that aided in my healing journey without me actually knowing at the time just how necessary they'd be. Remember these words: *care, connect, feel,* and *get help*—but in no particular order.

1. Engage in Self-Care

I see your eye roll. I know you have no time and likely no additional energy to spare. I'm not asking you to go work out for forty-five minutes a day. If one minute is all you have, then let's start there.

Assuming you have decent dental hygiene, I want you to take an extra sixty seconds after you brush your teeth each night to calm your nervous system. Close the door, and when you finish brushing, stand there at the sink for a minute longer than you normally would. Close your eyes and take a few slow, deep breaths.

If you have more than sixty seconds, there are so many other things you can do to practice self-care during your day.

My self-care during our cancer journey was usually practiced by writing, blogging, and throwing pop-up dance parties with my kids. My boys and I would yell at Alexa to play the

Disney Junior Dance Party playlist, and we would run around busting our killer moves all over the house. We still do this, and if the kids are in a cranky mood, it's the perfect reset for them, too. Even better than Disney Junior is screaming along to "Tubthumping" by Chumbawamba with them. This song also came on when I returned to the gym for the first time after Mike died. I was climbing the StairMaster, and it instantly gave me chills down my spine. Life's thrown me some pretty vicious curveballs, but so far, I've managed to get my butt back up each time. Now, every time my kids get a boo-boo, we sing it together.

Self-care might also look like spending just a few extra minutes outside in the fresh air. The outdoors is powerfully therapeutic. This is something we often forced upon Mike to give him a change of scenery—anything other than the walls of our living room. It had to be *very* warm outside, or we'd have to cover him in blankets, as Mike was almost *always* very cold. This was believed to be a side effect of his weight loss and his chemo medication.

Self-care might look like making your bed in the morning, taking a long warm shower, or cooking a healthy meal. It might be going for a walk, painting your nails, exercising, calling a friend, or getting lost in a show. My personal recommendation is *The Bachelor,* but to each their own.

Self-care is taking a few extra deep breaths when your head hits the pillow each night and finding things in life, despite all the tragedy, to still be grateful for. According to Harvard Health, practicing gratitude can actually lead to feelings of optimism and contentment in one's life and even help people better deal with adversity.[10]

Every single night when I'd ask myself what I was grateful for, all I could come up with was "my kids." With everything that was going wrong in my life, it was hard to feel gratitude for anything else. I'd tell myself that people had it worse—like that should make me feel better. But the truth was, my kids kept me grounded. The purpose of my gratitude practice wasn't to be creative. It was just me and, oftentimes, my children, with nobody else to judge my thoughts. I needed to be honest. Recognizing each night for even just sixty seconds how grateful I am for them gave me the nudge I needed to keep going.

I read a quote once that said something like, "If you're able to tuck your child into a warm bed in a safe house, you've won the lottery in life."[11] It made me realize that, despite it all, I'm still pretty damn fortunate.

Sixty seconds. Three deep breaths. One thing you're grateful for.

Leave a pen and notepad next to your bed, and as you get the hang of the practice, let your gratitude list grow. Share it on social media or, like Mike, keep it saved in the notes section of your phone. Keeping a gratitude journal is a wonderful form of self-care.

Whatever it is, do *something*, anything, that is for *you*.

2. Connect with Others

I cannot tell you how invaluable it is to connect with other people who can truly understand what you're going through. As I mentioned before, I searched and joined several Facebook communities for brain cancer patients and caregivers. The people in these groups spoke my language, a language that none of my friends or family could speak with me. They were facing the same barriers to care that we were. There were people further along in the disease who provided information that helped prepare me for what was to come. These groups rallied together and answered questions for each other, often in real time.

I connected with other widows on Instagram by searching popular hashtags like #widow, #widowhood, #youngwidow, #soloparent, #griefjourney, and #lifeafterloss. I found women with young children facing similar devastation as I was, sharing their pain but also their joys. Nothing has felt so relatable, and I'd never felt so understood.

Connect with others through your own story. Share what you went through or are currently going through in whatever format you want. Perhaps it's social media or a podcast, or maybe you want to write your *own* book. Your story deserves to be told. Your strength deserves to be recognized. And despite what you tell yourself, you can make a serious difference in someone's life when you share a story that can make them feel validated, which is what I hope this book does for you.

3. Feel Your Feelings

Make sure you give yourself time to grieve. Feel the feels. You're not weak if you cry. You're not heartless if you don't. You might be living in survival mode like I was, with very little time to let it all out. So, when you *are* feeling something, take a pause. Acknowledge how your body is feeling. Let it feel that way. Let out a scream, a cry, a sigh, or whatever it is you need. Maybe you can even create your own sad songs playlist.

Take a moment to see what your body needs before moving on to the next item on your to-do list. As a caregiver, this might require telling someone that you need a few minutes away. It took me a really long time to feel comfortable asking someone for that time. I felt like by taking a few minutes to myself, I was burdening someone else with *my* responsibilities. The truth is, though, people want to help.

Our feelings *need* to come out—in some way. Suppressing your feelings is a dangerous habit, and when you eventually can't suppress them any longer, which is a point you inevitably will reach, they will come out tenfold, affecting your own physical and mental health, as well as the health of your relationships. In fact, research suggests an association between suppressing emotions and an increased risk of chronic disease.[12]

Ride the grief waves as they come. Like my four-year-old often tells my three-year-old, *it is okay to cry.*

4. Get Help

You can't do it by yourself. You aren't meant to, and you shouldn't have to. I strongly believe that every single person can benefit from therapy. You don't need to be living through a crisis to just simply talk to someone who can help sort out your feelings and stressors day to day. Society has made incredible progress with the stigma around therapy, but we're still not *quite* there. I hope you leave this book knowing that there is absolutely no shame in therapy.

Know that it might take a couple of therapists to find the one that you really mesh with. Don't give up if you don't click with the first, second, or even the third therapist you meet with.

Sadly, our health system is not built to support mental health services right now. When I started going to therapy, my therapist kept giving me paperwork to submit to my insurance company because she was out of network, and I could only pay out of pocket. Fortunately, I had a lot of financial support that allowed me to continue therapy despite the insane inconvenience of it. The problem was, with the amount of paperwork and tracking I was already doing between Mike and my kids, I couldn't fathom filling out one more piece of paper. To physically fill out paperwork and have to mail it to my insurance company felt archaic and burdensome to someone who was already completely burned out every second of the day. I know I sound privileged saying that, but it's the truth. So, I paid $150 a visit for a few weeks and then told myself it was too expensive to continue. Not only was it too expensive, but the paperwork to get reimbursed was too much work, and for those reasons, I stopped seeing the therapist.

One day, I did a small poll on Instagram because I was curious if I was just being lazy or if other people felt the same way. Most people responded that they paid cash because their insurance didn't cover mental health services. Some didn't have the ability to be reimbursed, and others who did also felt like the burden of that reimbursement process was too outdated and cumbersome to deal with, just as I did.

That being said, if you can afford a therapist, that's wonderful. Sometimes, all you need are a few sessions. If you cannot find the time to attend therapy in person, know that most therapists have offered virtual options since COVID-19 hit. If you cannot afford therapy, you are absolutely not alone, and I'm sorry on behalf of America for that. There are more affordable options these days, such as Talkspace or BetterHelp, that you could start with. You could also inquire with your employer or (late) spouse's employer, as many employers offer an Employee Assistance Program for families that includes a set amount of free, confidential sessions with a licensed therapist over the phone.

I later returned to therapy, with and without my kids, seeing a therapist we lovingly refer to as our "feelings doctor." I know that my children's grief will develop in new ways over time as they reach new phases of their lives, and I want them to grow up believing that talking to a *feelings doctor* is anything but a weakness. I've come to better understand the range of emotions that I feel on a given day by talking to her, and she helps me to help my boys in their grief. Normalizing therapy for the next generation starts with us.

The same goes for appropriately prescribed medications. I used to think medication was a crutch that I was too strong to lean on. It meant I was weak—like the idea of medication challenged my ability to toughen up and deal with my problems myself. I mean, I was supposed to be a super-mom, damn it. I thought medication diminished my super-ness.

What a silly, uneducated thought process that was. I was on Zoloft daily and took Ativan as needed later on in Mike's illness. I've taken my Ativan more a year after his death than I did when he was sick. There is absolutely nothing wrong with using a little help from science. Medication can be situational, and it doesn't mean you have to depend on it or stay on it for the rest of your life. If you feel like you're struggling with your mental health, talk to your doctor to see if you're a good candidate for an antidepressant or anti-anxiety medication. A discussion with your doctor is always the *first step*.

There is *no* shame in getting help from a therapist or from your doctor. While I once thought it was a weakness, I now believe that taking steps to be in the best mental state I can be in for my family is superhero-level strength.

* * *

So, my friend, remember, you can do this. No matter where you are on your grief journey, you have the power to choose your next step. Let in the sadness and wholeheartedly embrace the joys. We're a team, and together, *we can keep growing and moving along through grief.*

Let's connect!

For partnerships, podcasts, and other speaking engagements or to just have a friend who *gets it*, subscribe to my website and connect with me at www.rebeccaditore.com. There, you'll find new blog posts on living life after loss and my "Grief, Myths, & Misconceptions" and "Your Next Steps in Grief" PDFs, along with all of my favorite grief-related resources, such as children's books, playlists, legacy projects, and more.

Come follow along with me on Instagram: @rebeccaditore.

Last, support the mental health of children who've lost a parent or sibling to cancer through my nonprofit organization, the Michael L. DiTore Small Moments Foundation. Learn more about our mission and how to get involved or make a donation at *www.smallmomentsfoundation.org*. For Small Moments-related inquiries, contact me at *rebecca@smallmomentsfoundation.org*.

Acknowledgments

To my dad, Bill. You have been my biggest supporter since the day I was born, whether it was cheering on the side of the basketball courts when I was a kid, running a half marathon by my side, or carrying me physically and emotionally through the loss of my husband as a young mom. Mike received the care that he did because I watched how you took care of mom first, and I am the mother I am today because of the father you've always been to me. Thank you for all the time you spent with the boys during Mike's illness and while I worked on this book. We appreciate everything you do for us.

To Debbie and Lou. Thank you for loving me like your own daughter and for everything you've done and continue to do for the boys and me. Thank you for raising Mike the way you did, molding him into the strong, brave, patient, loving man that I fell madly in love with. Thank you for being my teammates throughout this journey. I wouldn't be where I am today if it weren't for your ability to show up for us despite the unimaginable pain you feel every day. I feel so grateful.

To Nicole. You are the sister I never had growing up. I am so sorry for the pain you've endured. Sibling loss often goes unnoticed, but as I watch the undeniable bond grow between Dante and Dominic, I can better understand how very deep this cuts for you, and it's so unfair. Thank you for fighting through your own darkness to be a bright light for the boys. They love you. I love you.

To Matthew. I bet when you first added me on Instagram,

you didn't imagine me blasting your name in a book a year later. Thank you for your patience throughout this process and for your love and support. Thank you for seeing me as so much more than the trauma I've endured. You have made an unexpected and invaluable impact on our healing journey, and you've shown me that it's possible for my heart to expand and love again.

To the friends; family members; neighbors; and strangers who kept us in their thoughts and prayers or sent meals, gifts, and donations during Mike's cancer journey—you made us feel loved, and you eased some of the burden of cancer. It meant so much to our family, and I sincerely thank you.

Endnotes

1   Rosenfeld, Michael J., Reuben J. Thomas, and Maja Fal-
     con. 2018. How Couples Meet and Stay Together, Waves
     1, 2, and 3: Public version 3.04, plus wave 4 supplement
     version 1.02 and wave 5 supplement version 1.0 and wave 6
     supplement ver 1.0 [Computer files]. Stanford, CA: Stanford
     University Libraries. *https://data.stanford.edu/hcmst?_*
     ga=2.62621868.1203433893.1711132161-572989883.1711132161.

2   Cleveland Clinic, "Glioma," my.clevelandclinic.org, reviewed
     October 20, 2021. *https://my.clevelandclinic.org/health/diseas-*
     es/21969-glioma.

3   Kierstan Boyd, "What is Nystagmus?", American Academy of
     Ophthalmology, December 2, 2022. *https://www.aao.org/eye-*
     health/diseases/what-is-nystagmus#:~:text=Nystagmus%20
     Symptoms&text=Usually%20the%20movement%20is%20
     side,usually%20happens%20in%20both%20eyes.

4   Basinger H., Hogg JP. Neuroanatomy, Brainstem. [Updated
     2023 Jul 4]. In: StatPearls [Internet]. Treasure Island (FL): Stat-
     Pearls Publishing; 2024 Jan. *https://www.ncbi.nlm.nih.gov/*
     books/NBK544297/.

5   Zero Dean, *Lessons Learned from the Path Less Traveled*
     Volume 1: Get Motivated & Overcome Obstacles with Courage,
     Confidence & Self-Discipline, The Path Less Traveled Publishing,
     2018.

6   Mya Robarts, *The V Girl: A Coming of Age Story*, V Books, 2016.

7   Robert Breault, "In the happiest of our childhood memories, our parents were happy, too." AZ Quotes, accessed March 25, 2024. *https://www.azquotes.com/quote/615618*.

8   Robert Stigwood et al., *Grease*, Hollywood, CA, Paramount Pictures, 1978.

9   Graham Reynolds, PhD, "Toxic Positivity," Anxiety & Depression Association of America, September 23, 2022. *https://adaa.org/learn-from-us/from-the-experts/blog-posts/consumer/toxic-positivity*.

10   Harvard Health Publishing, "Giving Thanks Can Make You Happier," Harvard Medical School, August 14, 2021. *https://www.health.harvard.edu/healthbeat/giving-thanks-can-make-you-happier*.

11   Joe Flaherty (@josephflaherty), "If you're able to tuck in a healthy, peacefully sleeping child into a warm bed in a safe home, you've won the lottery in life." Twitter, October 2, 2020. *https://twitter.com/josephflaherty?lang=en*.

12   Chapman, B. P., Fiscella, K., Kawachi, I., Duberstein, P., & Muennig, P. (2013). Emotion suppression and mortality risk over a 12-year follow-up. Journal of Psychosomatic Research, 75(4), 381–385. *https://doi.org/10.1016/j.jpsychores.2013.07.014*.

Made in United States
Troutdale, OR
05/23/2024

20060180R00105